THE PEOPLE OF
THE CENTER

Carl F. Starkloff

THE PEOPLE OF
THE CENTER

AMERICAN INDIAN RELIGION
AND CHRISTIANITY

A CROSSROAD BOOK
The Seabury Press, New York

THE SEABURY PRESS
815 Second Avenue
New York, N.Y. 10017

Copyright © 1974 by Carl F. Starkloff
Designed by Elliot Epstein
Printed in the United States of America

Library of Congress Cataloging in Publication Data

Starkloff, Carl F
  The people of the center.

  (A Crossroad book)
  Bibliography: p. 142
  1. Indians of North America—Religion and mythology.   2. Indians of North America—Missions.
3. Christianity.   I. Title.
E98.R3S73   299'.7   73-17885
  ISBN 0-8164-9207-7

To
The
Native
Americans

At the center of the earth
I stand,
Behold me
At the wind center
I stand,
Behold me,
A root of herb.
Therefore I stand,
At the wind center
I stand.

Song of the Sacred Pole,
Teton Sioux Sun Dance

Preface

From the beginning, it is important to emphasize *for whom* I am writing, and who might stand to gain from reading this book. I refer to white Americans, and especially white Christians, who may have less knowledge and understanding of Indian tradition than I have. Indian Americans might choose to read this book and, if they do, one hopes they will not find that it always describes a stranger—and yet this will inevitably happen, since I know well enough that I am not one of those who "really understand Indians." Such a claim is always a generalization beyond any one person's experience, and would differ little from a statement about "White Americans" from a reference point in Brooklyn, Milwaukee, or Seattle.

I am not an anthropologist, although I have read extensively in the works of various scholars. If this work is to make any original contribution, it will be as a study in religion by one who has grasped the fact that his human resources are after all the most important, and just as valuable as theological and ecclesiastical literature. Therefore, the data for this book are both documentary and personal, and the "theological reflection" is my own. The reader will find my academic sources listed in the Bibliography, which is only a small part of an overwhelming list of available and not-so-available works. Personal sources come out of my own history among the Indian people. This includes the good fortune of having spent two years as a Jesuit seminarian, teaching, driving school buses, coaching, working with my hands, and simply being among Indians on the reservation in Wyoming. It also includes two years as a chaplain to the Indian students from all over the United States who attended Haskell American Indian College in Lawrence, Kansas, as well as part-time assistance to the Prairie Band Pottawotomi in eastern Kansas. More recently I have also come to know many urban Indians of the "diaspora" in the Kansas City area, and to share some of their aspirations for cultural, political, and economic recognition.

The method here will entail guarding against the ever-present danger of overgeneralization, especially the facile use of the term "the Indian," while at the same time trying to present areas in which one might with some assurance draw valid general conclusions and spiritual insight. As an aid to this procedure, I employ the basic categories of Ninian Smart for the study and evaluation of religions,[1] according to the way in which they meet the mythical, doctrinal, ethical, social, ritual, and experiential dimensions of human life. In some cases I have seen fit to telescope these categories by using Joachim Wach's framework of the creedal, cultic, and communal-moral aspects of religion.

It remains for me to express my gratitude to a number of people. First of all, I thank the many Indian people who have assisted me and shown me hospitality and friendship, along with friendly criticism. I thank my own family for their constant encouragement in all that I do. I also express appreciation to my Jesuit superiors and school officials at Rockhurst College for providing me with financial help as well as summers free from teaching obligations.

[1] Cf. *The Religious Experience of Mankind* (New York: Charles Scribner's Sons, 1969).

Contents

Chapter One

"Those Old Indians Knew . . ."

THE MYTHICAL AND DOCTRINAL DIMENSIONS, 21

Chapter Two

Celebration

THE RITUAL DIMENSION, 51

Introduction

Then Nih'a^{n}ca^n gave the Arapaho the middle part of the earth to live in.[1]

ARAPAHO CREATION MYTH

And the Lord God planted a garden in Eden, in the east; and there he put the man whom he had formed.

GENESIS 2:8

There is no religious tradition that does not try to understand the Myth of the Center. Each individual possesses that sense of alienation which tells him at least subconsciously of a lost integrity, while every society somehow mythologizes that Golden Age, the time of wholeness, and man's search for it. It is with some appreciation of this sense of estrangement that the white Christian should approach the traditional experience of his fellow Americans, his elder brothers and sisters who inhabited this hemisphere thousands of years before his own ancestors, and to whose present social and religious alienation those ancestors often contributed. By understanding their own separation from what they would like to be, and by examining the divisions in their own society and religious environment, Whites can become empathetic sharers in the Indian's individual, social, and religious situation. Seeking the same destiny, as

[1] George A. Dorsey and Alfred L. Kroeber, *Traditions of the Arapaho* (Chicago: Field Columbian Museum, Publication 81, Anthropological Series, Vol. V, October, 1903), p. 48.

we all are, under different images—that is, our true selves, wholeness, oneness with God—we cannot afford premature judgments and cultural prejudices that might close us to others.

The first caution that a writer must observe in the study of Native American culture, providing he has overcome the grosser prejudices of racial and cultural defensiveness, is to shun sentimentality. I do not believe in the "noble savage"—that he ever existed or ever will at any moment in created time. There have always been and still are unattractive and even disturbing facets to Indian tribal life and religious practices, just as there are in inner-city South Chicago, in Scarsdale and Beverly Hills, and in the great traditions of Asian and European religion. Which of these traditions has shown a greater dominance of such negative traits is a moot point. Suffice it to say that anyone who has worked any length of time among Indian people, rural or urban, experiences sharply conflicting feelings about "the Indian problem." For such persons it is no mere academic exercise to ask such questions as: Should Indians assimilate into American society? Can reservation life be converted into a viable cultural milieu, that is, into an environment where culture, the overarching design of a people's life, can thrive? Is primitive tribal tradition a hindrance to Indian well-being? . . . A firsthand knowledge of reservation life often leads one to brood over the pathetic and angry outcry for a new recognition of and respect for Indian cultural integrity. For with whatever improvements the white man's culture may have brought to the Indians, it has also brought about the barren reservation, bewilderment leading to inertia and idleness, cultural and religious schizophrenia, and very often a pervasive tone of despair. No doubt this book will often reflect such a paradoxical mood of admiration for the beauties of the Indian ideal side by side with depression at the present situation.

One newly recognized catalyst in the present willingness of white Americans and white Christians to reexamine Indian culture favorably is a discovery of the relativity of white middle-class values and cultural forms. There is a new kind of poverty of spirit in the air that has been made apparent by the various counter-cultural movements, and by an awakened sense of the absence of cultural identity in so much of white Christian America, now long severed from its European roots. This new humility, where it exists, leads to a reassessment of the problem of "assimilation" and of the melting-pot theory. There is a new openness to the great values that lie at some level of Native American life: the deep religious instincts and symbolism, the sense of solidarity with creation, the primitive and profound philosophies of life, the unique gifts of personal and social integrity. If, in becoming familiar with Indian traditions, we feel some kind of vague nostalgia, it may be that we are experiencing some of that longing for a primitive wholeness that all humanity desires. It is not perhaps a futile sentimentality, but rather, what Hartley Burr Alexander referred to as the recognition of common elements in the human spirit, shared by all peoples regardless of geographical and chronological boundaries.

The non-Indian who seeks to learn about the Indian religious tradition is in for stern schooling, both in the areas to which he is introduced and in the resistance he receives. The basic reason for this lies in the nature of a cultural religion: this is not a missionary religion but a sacred tribal gnosis not intended for outsiders, who are presumed to have their own ways of worshiping. Second, there is the distaste that Indians now have for endless analysis by anthropologists and social scientists, whether these have the genuine interest of the Indian at heart or not. Last, after so many years of rejection, of repression of their own language in white schools, of ridicule of Indian rituals in the name of Christian superiority, Indians find it hard to trust a white Christian who is sincerely interested in dialogue. Even when the Indian recognizes such genuineness, he will tend to guard his knowledge closely and consider it highly privileged, because this possession is almost the only one that Whites have not been able to expropriate along with the land, the waters, and the wildlife. If a White does enter into any form of conversation, he must do it as a learner, a beneficiary, even as a beggar.

Such an interested Christian will be well advised to reach into his own tradition and become aware of that alien element within that we call "sin." In this case, sin is defensiveness and fear of what is strange and new—the sin of the closed mind. Such sin will often justify itself by a blind "ideology"—the strong and perhaps passionate espousal of a certain world-view or dogmatic position. There is nothing per se evil in ideology; to some extent all people need something of the sort if they are to live with enthusiasm and vigor. But when a dogma or a creed or a myth so dominates our consciousness that we can no longer be attentive, intelligent, reasonable, and responsible, it constitutes the disorder that the Bible describes as sin. In persons so affected, there is no capacity for self-transcendence, for the searching out of a common meaning with other men that is basic to community.

Let me propose a stance for the non-Indian Christian in relation to the Indian's struggle for social and religious liberation. To begin with, the White must inevitably be an outsider to Indian culture, especially in its religious aspects.

When he comes seeking understanding or experience, he is, as I have said, a mendicant. Indian religion demands detailed initiation even for its own, and full familiarity is never granted to non-Indians, even those most trusted. Again, this Indian reserve is not intended to give offense; it is simply the Indians' conviction that heaven has entrusted this version of the "mystery" to them for safekeeping.

Nevertheless, there is an important place for the "outsider" among oppressed or alienated cultures as they move toward self-determination. Black theologian J. Deotis Roberts, taking a more conciliatory attitude than James Cone, believes that there is a place for Whites in Black liberation. I would suggest that his explanation also applies to the relation between Whites and Indians. While Cone has maintained that only the oppressed themselves can write their own theology of liberation, Roberts holds that it *is* possible to study a faith-claim from the outside as well as from the inside. He believes that an exclusively internal study may often be too subjective to be open to critical evaluation.

Indian leader Vine Deloria, Jr., has stated that the best thing the national denominations of Christianity can do to help revitalize Indian mission work is to assist in the creation of a national Indian Christian Church. This kind of church would incorporate all existing missions and programs into one national church to be entirely in the hands of Indian people. Such a proposal, however near or far from realization, corresponds with the traditional missionary principle that foreigners should ultimately leave an area in the hands of "native clergy." Assumed here is the transformation of cultural forms of worship from those brought in by missionaries into forms more congenial to local attitudes and needs. Christian Indians could then worship the God of Christianity as their own High God rediscovered, and not in the alien forms of Roman, German, or New England social structures. If the gospel of Jesus Christ does not restrict itself to any one cultural expression—and this is one of the meanings of justification by faith!—then Christianity must fit into a multitude of cultural forms. Transcendence does not necessarily mean negation. As Deloria has commented, "I think the New Testament is really a mirror in which each culture looks to see if it's really there."

Separatism for its own sake is not the goal of Christian Indians; they seek, rather, a deeper penetration of Christianity into areas where, because of missionaries' lack of imagination or knowledge, the Church has never gone. What they generally envisage is an ethnic church community of common meaning, able ultimately to relate to other church groups on the basis of an even wider common meaning. Like the Black Power movement, Deloria's "More Real Involvement for Indians" aims at an attainment of independence and personal recognition from which to carry on a dialogue with Whites wherein all parties are treated as having something to contribute and to learn.

White Christians thus have a provisional role in Indian worship and its evolution, the role of cross-cultural facilitators in the Indian search for a relevant spiritual life. As we shall note later in this book, there is already a great deal of evidence for Christianity's having played such a role in the preservation of tribal practices. But a cross-cultural relationship must be two-way. I think it is safe to say that White Americans, too—perhaps to an even greater degree in many cases—are culturally deprived people. Indians, on the other hand, are more materially deprived and socially estranged, but within their tradition is a rich culture that still lives in the memories of the old people, and with the help of these memories we can retrieve the genuine tribal mythos.

As an individual, I confess to being driven to this work partly by a need to make amends for a certain obtuseness to Indian values and a naïve acceptance of middle America, giving scant attention to the thought that these ways are not suited for other social groups. In this, I think that I was much of America and many Christian bodies in microcosm. Collectively, we must lift more than that "one finger" demanded by Jesus to remove such burdens from other shoulders. Without despising or feeling inferior about our own backgrounds—we cannot work in freedom with such an attitude—we might take our cue from Black Elk, the Oglala Sioux holy man who bequeathed his legacy to John G. Neihardt and Joseph Epes Brown. Black Elk came to see that if his own vision of himself as saviour of his people was to become a reality, he would have to place his charge in the hands of trustworthy men of the dominant culture. Men such as Neihardt and Brown are most cautious about any glib allusions to "bringing civilization to savages," and they are eager to aid Indian people in retaining what is vital and life-giving in their traditions. The giving of life can work two ways—for Whites as well as for Indians.

By way of a brief addendum, I might note how American history records a tragic caricature of the meeting of Christianity and Indian tradition, a syncretic religio-social movement in which a visionary messiah figure stood forth in place of the Christ of the New Testament, and a frantic apocalyptic crowded out the last glimmers of Christian hope. Genuine leadership on the part of the churches should have prevented this event by the proclamation and practice of the prayer of Christ that all may be one. The message of the Scriptures might have stood forth as the sign of a great future for all races. Instead, the few shreds and tatters of Christianity that did remain in the Indian consciousness became merely a means for an attempted return to the Golden Age when the buffalo were plentiful and the land was free and unpolluted by mines and railroads. Human beings cannot live merely in the present. If they have no vision, they perish by their own attempts to return to a better time, which of course looks better than the misery of the moment.

This convergence of two lines of belief, as many readers will recognize, took place somewhere in Nevada in the ecstatic experience of one Jack Wilson, a Paiute Indian better known to history as Wovoka. This visionary prophet suddenly appeared on the scene with a message that he had been taken up to heaven and had seen a magnificent revelation of salvation for the oppressed and despairing Indians and the demise of the white intruder. Some say that Wovoka did not claim to be the messiah but merely a forerunner of the Christ, who was soon to return and restore all the good things of ancient Indian life. In any case, there began the movement known as the Ghost Dance, a harmonization of the Indian's love for a land he held sacred and of Christian and late Jewish apocalyptic which promised the resurrection of the dead and the destruction of evildoers.

There was much that was beautiful about this movement. Wovoka counseled Indians to remain nonviolent, to be faithful to family life, to pray and hope, and above all, to dance. They were to dance that ecstatic circular dance about the center of life, singing those songs of supplication that now remain to posterity in some contemporary peyote rites. Even more impressive was the exhortation for all Indians to come together, to cease fighting among themselves—a message of truly prophetic ethical value, for Indian tribes too had a long record of strife and warfare over hunting grounds and other, less significant causes. Maybe here, for the first time in active memory, Indians would truly be one people.

But, as is only too well known, the movement was doomed to that same fate suffered by Jewish zealotry in Jerusalem as it struggled, though more violently, to drive out the foreign intruder. The Ghost Dance spread like a grass fire eastward, southward, and northward; more elaborate myths sprang up along with it, such as the idea that the Ghost Dance shirt would ward off the white man's bullets and that a great flood would engulf the white men as it engulfed all creation in the dawn celebrated by Indian mythology. But the vision came to a crashing halt under the Hotchkiss guns of a panicky and no doubt vengeance-bound army detachment at Wounded Knee Creek, in South Dakota, in late December of 1890. Hartley Burr Alexander writes of how a Sioux woman took up the Ghost Dance shirt worn by an Indian killed in the warfare, with the piteous and symbolic complaint, "They told me it would stop the bullets. But it is no good. I do not want it. Throw it away." It was the end of a tradition of millennia lost to memory.

And still, it is to this point, or shortly prior to it, somewhere in the early nineteenth century, that I am suggesting we look to find an opening to achieve for all Americans what the Ghost Dance strove for vaguely and with confusion. We must try to restore the spirit of hope that sees

humankind of every tribe and tongue and nation assem-
bled before the throne. Some current Indian movements
evince a desire for this, and white and Indian leaders are
trying to join the spirit of Indian vision-quest, Christian
prophecy, and the peyote cult in a search for global unity.
We can read many Indian religious lodge prayers that, although lamenting the Indian lot, also pray that all may
live together in peace. My own experience of reservation
social and religious gatherings is of an intense desire to be
at one with other tribes and white people. This is especially
true of the Sun Dance in some instances, where Christian
elements have already entered and transformed much of
the ceremony, or where Christian clergymen are invited
to give opening invocations. For the most part, Indians are
willing to return to the early spirit of hospitality that existed
between Indians and Whites as we read of it in early New
England accounts and in the records of the explorations
of Europeans in the eighteenth and nineteenth centuries.
If, along with this spirit, we can develop a Christianity
grounded in Indian culture or encourage a dialogue between the two, we may still be able to gain from the best
of two ancient worlds.

Chapter One

"Those Old Indians Knew..."

THE MYTHICAL AND DOCTRINAL DIMENSIONS

I stood here, I stood there,
The Clouds are speaking,
I say, "You are the ruling power,
I do not understand, I only know what I am told,
You are the ruling power, you are now speaking,
This power is yours, O heavens."

> *Song of Man-Chief*, as Tirawa spoke
> in the clouds—Pawnee[1]

. . . close behind and close in front you fence me round,
shielding me with your hand.
Such knowledge is beyond my understanding,
a height to which my mind cannot attain.

> Psalm 139:5–6, JERUSALEM BIBLE

The more secular knowledge man acquires, the more man seems to develop a curiosity, if not an anxiety, for the sacred. The different secularizing movements in the churches, valuable as they have been in some respects, have nearly

---

[1] Frances Densmore, *Pawnee Music* (Washington, D.C.: Government Printing Office, 1929), Smithsonian Institution, Bureau of American Ethnology Papers, Bulletin 93, p. 88. These volumes will be cited henceforth as *S. I.*

always ended with a new search for mystery and wonder. It may be that man no longer believes that God truly dwells atop Sinai, or that His voice is the thunderclap. And yet, the longing he has to find the source of his being and to experience a spiritual wholeness finally comes to the foreground of consciousness, leading him persistently into those fantasies and myths that might interpret for him the unknown. As Carl G. Jung maintained, a society that has lost its capacity for myth is like a man who has lost his soul.

When we speak of "the primitive," we ought literally to take off our shoes. If we lightly dismiss all elements of the supernatural with such a term, intending it to mean any quality that belongs to a benighted, bygone age or a backward society, we sadly misconceive ourselves and our own world. The notion of the primitive is not chronological or geographical, but existential: it explains those hidden forces in individuals and collectivities that call for expression and interpretation. Witnessing today's resurgence of witchcraft, demonology, drug-culture transcendence, bizarre ritualism, and a new interest in mysticism, it is only prudent at least to suspect that the primitive is deep within each one of us. To be sure, this area needs careful discernment, but it also demands reverence.

Werner Mueller has pointed out that the traditional Indian search for visions is based on just such a reverence. That is, the Indians' need for a cosmology—a coherent explanation of their world—made them realize the limitations of mere dogmatic statements and impelled them to develop a more convincing understanding of religious knowledge and revelation. Modern science too, even in its most empiricist forms, has come to see itself as working within an atmosphere of mystery, and man still turns to trans-scientific means of truly knowing his world, or having a *kosmos,* the whole and ordered world sought by ancient philosophers of every culture.

Within this search for a cosmology we discover one reason why the projections of many earlier anthropologists with regard to Indian religious forms have not been fully realized, indeed have even been refuted. When some of the most reputable scholars predicted the demise of the Sun Dance and other such rituals, they were no doubt looking too much to the external forces of history such as military power and legal sanction, and not enough to the needs of the human spirit and the persistence of the mythical consciousness. If the stubborn attachment to ancient beliefs and rites has remained so strong among Indians, we might now suggest that the dominant white culture in America encourages this attachment. If Indian religious culture *is* doomed to extinction—though I see no conclusive reason why it must bow to that sentence—we should allow it to die its own evolutionary death rather than the death of a white impostor acting like an Indian. If Indian forms of worship are to disappear, they should be allowed to pass gradually into other forms, and not be suppressed by edict or ridicule. For Indians who are also Christians, the possession of such culture may eventually make their Christianity far more vibrant and spirit-filled than that of a more "sophisticated" society.

We know that myth—and by myth I mean simply articulations of the mysterious in story and symbol—precedes doctrinal statement. Likewise, there is no systematic arrangement of teaching and dogma in tribal religion which is separate from symbolic presentation in ritual settings. It is simply for pedagogical purposes that I am arranging Indian beliefs in doctrinal form *before* going into their mythological and ritual origins.

One other caveat is important here. It is very difficult so to analyze much of Indian culture as to be able to separate out what is distinctively Indian and what derives from white Christian influence, what might be a transformation brought about by missionaries or by Indian religious leaders themselves. For the present practical needs of Indian religious life, the distinction is mostly academic. After all, modern Christian practices and forms of expression are combinations of primitive kerygma, early teachings surrounding it, and local cultures. However, in order to indicate the uniqueness of the Amerindian tradition, I shall try to isolate the Native American and the European Christian wherever this is possible.

It can be said of nearly every tribe of North America that there are certain religious beliefs ("doctrines" in the loose sense indicating traditions passed on by instruction given during sacred rites) contained in their various mythologies. It is interesting to note that there does seem to exist a deep strain of agnosticism among some tribes—in the case of the Comanche nearly the entire culture—relating to a supreme being, to immortality, and to the existence of spirits. Such a strain may be attributable to the warlike and highly mobile nature of this tribe, for which a word like "nomadic" would be gross understatement. The early efforts of Franciscan missionaries to introduce Christianity and domesticity among these people finally failed. Again, among some of the southwest tribes one finds a vagueness about the existence of one supreme deity, even though other aspects of religious life and belief are exceptionally rich. Such tribes, like the different Pueblo peoples, seem actually to have relied much more on elaborate ritual than on any doctrinal statements.

The majority of North American tribes, however, have

maintained some kind of faith in the High God through the activities relating to Him. Always allowing for variations from tribe to tribe or nation to nation, and for the inevitable obfuscations in interpretation, one may schematize Indian beliefs in (1) the High God as Creator, Maker, or Spirit, (2) intermediary divinities, (3) creation, (4) eschatology or "last things," and (5) an elaborate cosmology affecting the whole range of religious activities.

THE HIGH GOD

As we have noted, most North American Indian tribes profess some belief in a supreme deity; indeed, Indians themselves usually expostulate vehemently with those who might hint that such belief is essentially a Christian contribution to their religon. The degree to which this High God is recognized in ceremonial and practical living varies in different tribes. For instance, the Creator receives attention under various titles and functions in many plains Indian origin myths, but practically none in the stories told around campfires, save for an occasional bit of speculation that some hero might be symbolic of the Father. There is, of course, an analogy here to the differences between religious myth and fairy tale in all folk literature.

It is only equitable to point out that a number of scholars have strongly denied any monotheistic belief among Indians, though such assertions are often oversimplified; just as some Christians have tended to oversimplify such concepts as "noble savage" and "the soul naturally Christian." Edwin Thompson Denig, for example, in his experience with the Crow Indians in the early nineteenth century found no civilized form of religion and no belief in God or immortality.[2] Denig was, it should be noted, more an explorer and trader than a scholar, however sympathetic he intended to be. Similarly, the more recognized anthropologist Garrick Mallery also wrote that, while Indians are an elaborately religious people, they are definitely not monotheistic. Any such assertion of a supreme Great Spirit or First Cause would be imputing to Indians a philosophy not attained prior to European influence.[3]

Even with Mallery, it is important to question whether his understanding of language and his own mental categories restricted what he was able to glean from Indian lore and evidence about a "First Cause" or personal God. (Theologians like Karl Barth would tell Mallery that Europeans are no better off philosophically in relation to God than their primitive friends in America and Africa.) But one must take even more seriously a linguistic philosopher like Ernst Cassirer, who held that the reactions of early missionaries to Indian identifications of the biblical God with an aboriginal High Deity were naïve and precipitate. Cassirer thought that this identification was due to many Indians' pragmatic desire at that time for acceptance by Whites. Cassirer's theory of Indian languages assumed that such deities as the Dakota Wakanda and Algonquian Manito were merely aggregates of world Powers rather than personal deities, and that missionaries were romanticizing when they identified such deities with the Judeo-Christian God.

---

[2] E. T. Denig, "Of the Crow Nation," S. I., Bulletin 151 (1953). No. 33, pp. 1–74; see p. 59.
[3] Garrick Mallery, in S. I., Tenth Annual Report, ed. J. W. Powell (1893), p. 491.

Granting the likelihood that the entire truth about this argument will never be known, published evidence among anthropological works in favor of primitive monotheism far outweighs evidence against it. Moreover, the present realization of the widely varied understandings of Godhead behind different Old Testament names should lead one to be cautious of embracing simplistic pictures of a personal God, intelligible to the human mind. After all, when Moses requested the voice from the burning bush to tell him its name, he received an answer to the effect ˙(and Scripture tells us even here that it was the voice of a messenger): "Never mind what my name is. Do what I tell you!" And still the Israelites came to address God in highly personal terms. So too, to some extent according to various Indian traditions, the old Indians had a personal idea of the same God, who entered into the rituals and whose primitive archetypal image dwelt deep within the Indian soul.

Thus, belief in such a High God, however distant, is evident among early Algonquians of the northeastern United States and Canada, and among the so-called Five Civilized Tribes ("civilized" because Whites found them farming and stable, with detailed governmental apparatus): Cherokee, Seminole, Creek, Chickasaw, and Choctaw. Indeed, the Seminole had a spiritual conception of God as the one "who makes everybody's breath" but lives far off and sends a human or semidivine intermediary named este-fas-ta to aid the people. Louis Capron found this belief prominent in the Green Corn Dance among the Seminole who had not submitted to Christian missionary influence even by the first half of this century.[4] Capron also observed among

[4] Louis Capron, "The Medicine Bundles of the Florida Seminole and the Green Corn Dance," S. I., Bulletin 151 (1953), No. 35, pp. 155–210, esp. pp. 172–174. The various Green Corn dances were rites of propitia-

them a highly sophisticated idea of praying to sa-kee-tom-mas-see, not so as to persuade Him of something but rather to make the one praying truly aware of Him. In the western United States, we find writings and testimonies to monotheism among the widely scattered Siouan, western Algonquian, and Caddoan peoples, as well as among the Shoshone tribes and some of the Athabascan groups whose history stretches from Alaska to New Mexico.

Personal conversation with contemporary Indian people has revealed conceptions of God as Earth Maker, Our Maker, Our Father, Creator, Giver, Man-Above, Great Holy, Master (or Lord) of Life—all of these pointing to a primitive cosmological notion of the divine activity. As one scholar pointed out about the Shoshone, the God they know today and identify with primitive notions certainly approximates the biblical God, but it would be rash to assert that this is nothing but a Christian contribution.[5] Moreover, direct reception of this idea from Christianity would produce a closer correspondence in terminology unless there were already some indigenous notion present in the Indian mentality. Such names as those listed above would seem to be of Indian origin, and would have prompted an affirmative response to the white missionary's talk of the God of the patriarchs and of Jesus Christ.

An old story is related about an Inca chieftain of the high civilization who was known for his deep religious nature.

---

tion, celebrated over several days of fasting, dancing, prayer, and judicial activity. Through these dances, God would send new life for the tribe and the individual, giving it into the Medicine Bundle, and the people could again eat the green corn, symbolic of life.

[5] D. B. Shimkin, "The Wind River Shoshone Sun Dance," S. I., Bulletin 151 (1953), No. 41, pp. 397–484, esp. p. 423. Comparisons and contrasts of this ceremony with the Arapaho Sun Dance will be made later.

The beginning of his religious conversion is traced to the moment when, in the early evening, he stood gazing under his cupped hand into the setting sun. His high priest remonstrated with him that to stare at the sun was blasphemous. The story goes that the king said to the priest:

"I have a question to ask you: Is it not true that I am your king and sovereign?"

"Certainly, master," replied the priest.

"And if I should order you to undertake a long journey for me across this land or even over the sea, you would obey me?"

"You are my lord, and I would obey."

"Then does it not seem to you that this great god, the sun, as he journeys day after day across the heavens, vanishing by night and returning by morning, would sometimes stop his travels and rest unless he were obeying a greater master than himself?"

Whatever its grounding in historical fact, the story symbolizes what might have been the American Indians' slow dawning of a God-consciousness, of a belief in one Lord.

There is no doubt that when present-day worshipers at the various Sun Dance ceremonies salute the rising sun with their solemn rites, they are recalling a time centuries ago when the sun was conceived as the highest god. But the Indians generally insist that their awakening to monotheism went on long before the Christians came; and there is no serious reason to deny that their intelligence could recognize the Creator from the things that are made, as St. Paul said of the Gentiles. It would simply be another example of what we might call, with Carl G. Jung, the archetypal experience of divinity and fatherhood. It would be impossible to relate all the traditions that point in this direction, but it will be valuable here to examine some examples of the place of God as Creator in Indian myth.

My own experience of an Indian account of divine creative activity comes from conversations. Countless times in past years Indians have told me of their belief in one God long before the missionaries arrived, and of how they so readily adopted Christianity because of this. The men and women of my own acquaintance would have been the children and grandchildren of those tribal leaders who first accepted Christianity as the fulfillment of their own tribal beliefs. More recently I have heard tribespeople affirm of the Sun Dance: "Some people think we worship the sun. This is false. We worship the Creator of the sun through the sun." In discussion with various Arapaho people, it was learned that the ancient tribal name for God is Chebeniatha^n or Ichebeniatha^n, to give only two of many ways of spelling it in English, and it means literally, "Man-Above," or "White- [i.e., shining] Man-Above." Arapaho distinguish between this name and the name they later applied to Christian teaching and used in the Lord's Prayer, Ba-he-nes-anani, or simply Heisanani, the ordinary word for "father." This most likely comes from the verb *ne-h'nes-thiit*, suggesting the bond between God as Father and as Creator. As in other strongly religious cultures, there are many names for God, such as Bä-thä-äth, or "holy one," a title applied to a blessed spirit before Christian teaching brought in the Holy Ghost, whom the Arapaho named Bä-tä-än, "the Holy One."

As far back as 1902 George Dorsey and the great Alfred Kroeber—then Dorsey's junior colleague—recorded the name of God, first, as Chebeniatha, the one to whom Sun Dance vows are made, second, as Heisanin, meaning "Our Father" but not indicating this to be of Christian origin,

and third, Hixtcäbä Nih'a^{n}ca^n. The latter is a mysterious
term that may reveal much about mythical thinking. Kroeber and Dorsey saw the name to be the one the Arapaho
gave to the Christian God, because it meant "above-white-
man." [6] However, further study has led me to wonder if
perhaps this name was simply another version of Ichebeni-
atha^n, referring to some myths about the apotheosis of the
ancient tribal hero Nih'a^{n}ca^n, whose name today is generally pronounced "Niatha$^{n''}$" and is also applied to any white
person. Very significantly this would, if verifiable, take the
name back prior to Christianity and link it with the creation story. Sister Inez Hilger, while doing her painstaking
study among the northern Arapaho, learned also that the
word pronounced *niatha* can also mean "spider," a creature
that has always inspired a sense of wonder among primi-
tives and "moderns" alike. [7] Here any possible identification
between God and a spider would refer to the mysterious
ways in which Providence and its natural manifestations
work. Most Arapaho, however, deny that there was any
literal identification between the deity and a spider. What
all this information indicates, in its sometimes tedious com-
plexity, is a very involved tradition about the existence and
nature of God. It seems clear that created phenomena, since
they possess spiritual qualities, often led the Arapaho to
some sense of the existence of a Creator.

There is an abundance of other evidence for this primitive monotheism. The Delaware Big House ceremony is
primarily a commemoration of man's place in the World

[6] Dorsey and Kroeber, *Traditions of the Arapaho* (Chicago: Field
Columbian Museum, Publication 81, Anthropological Series, Vol. V,
October, 1903), pp. 1–49.

[7] Sister M. Inez Hilger, *Arapaho Child Life and Its Cultural Background,* S. I., Vol. 148 (1952), pp. 144–145.

House, where he prays to the Creator for preservation. Among many Indian societies, whenever a great hero appears, he is first a human power, initially subjected to powers above, then taken into heaven and given divine powers. But whenever there is a hint of many divine powers, contemporary Indians affirm both that one Power stands behind all of these and commands them, and that this is an ancient Indian belief. Corresponding evidence gleaned within African cultures gives strength to this position.

No doubt much of this verbal sparring over the names of God would provoke the response that Dee Brown records of Chief Joseph of the Nez Percé, when he refused an offer of Christian churches and schools. The great leader feared that such establishments would only teach his people how to quarrel about God. Indians might quarrel with other men over things on this earth, he said, but they never want to quarrel about God.

Perhaps the clearest representation of the nature of this widespread pre-Christian monotheism is an account given by a Chippewa medicine man to Inez Hilger: The Supreme Being—Kícē Măn'ito or Great Spirit—always existed for the Chippewa as the giver of life. But He was far away, and not often addressed in prayer and ritual, except at the great Mide-wiwin celebration. As among the ancient Hebrews, His name, if spoken at all, was uttered with hushed reverence. Generally the Indians prayed to the various powers of nature for their immediate needs, and began praying directly to God only after Christian instruction. But God was always thought of as being "up there" and ready to be addressed by man.[8]

[8] Sister M. Inez Hilger, *Chippewa Child Life and Its Cultural Background*, S. I., Vol. 146 (1951), p. 60.

My own reaction to this kind of evidence points to a rediscovery of a new approach to "natural theology," or signals of the divine emanating from creation to man, as Peter Berger describes in his *A Rumor of Angels*. If Christians are no longer able to feel secure with "proofs" of God's existence from scientific arguments, they will be rewarded richly by observing these less clear-cut but still powerful signs in primitive human nature pointing to the One who must sustain man lest he cease to be.

DIVINE INTERMEDIARIES AND DEMIGODS

The Jewish and Moslem traditions have always insisted that God needs no mediator, but is intimately close to humankind and loves it. Yet, even in these religions there are accounts of angels and divine messengers who speak to man for God, apparently because men may find the presence of divinity too awesome to bear. To whatever degree the believer may wish to be friendly with God, he always acknowledges that God is holy, and that there is a *tremendum* about His presence. This awareness seems in general to be the Indian attitude. It is possible that this sense of awe made it more natural for Indians in many cases to identify so quickly and closely with Jesus Christ, to acknowledge His presence through rites added to the Sun Dance, the Peyote Tipi, the Sweat Lodge, and other services of worship. The figure of a holy mediator is very real to these people, and for Christian Indians today, Christ has become "the one mediator between God and men," symbolized by different forces in nature and ritual like the Thunderbird and the Lodge Pole. It is an attitude encouraged by St. Paul, who could both insist on the uniqueness of Jesus Christ as mediator and still speak reverently of the created powers on earth and in the heavens, as they profess their subjection to Him.

In most tribal religions, the highest mediator is a human-like figure, or culture-hero. This hero is often also a "trick-ster," playing all sorts of mischievous pranks, being in turn made a fool of, and even getting involved in obscene affairs. Yet he represents the power of good as well as evil, and bears within his person the paradoxes of nature, human and nonhuman, as well as the more paradoxical signs of the workings of Providence.

The trickster may be an explanation of the arbitrariness of natural phenomena and a combination of Eros and Pan. Among the Seminole, there is the figure of este fas-ta, the mediator for sa-kee-tom-mas-see, the far-off God who makes everybody's breath. Many students of Indian mythology think the Algonquian Manito is more an apotheosized hero than the ultimate High God, since he works in the form of a demiurge, or intermediary of divine power. The Sioux speak of a son of the Creator known for many ages. Whether this is actually a Christian addition is not clear, but the famous Dakota Sioux myth of the coming of the White Buffalo Woman to protect the nation and bestow the Sacred Pipe indicates a definite belief in the Supreme Being who sends messengers to do His bidding. Hartley Burr Alexander writes of the myths of the southwest, which tell of the many personified powers present at the creation-dawn—like the Old Testament personifications of Wis-dom, "there at the making of the world" (see Wisdom, ch. 9).

Among the northern and southern Arapaho we find tales of Found-in-Grass and Blood-Clot-Boy, wonder babies discovered by old women and raised by them. Found-in-Grass later develops into another tribal hero and becomes symbolic of the Creator and Giver of the Sacred Bundle, for the Supreme Being has everything good in His bag for the people. We also find in this same tradition the many tales involving the aforementioned Nih'a^{n}ca^n, the tribal hero called "Shining-White-Man." Of course, the name also later came to mean "spider" and was applied, often no doubt derisively, to all Whites. My suspicion that this figure also enters into the name of High God, besides being scientifically suspect, received a setback when I asked an elderly Indian about the White-Man-Above and White-Man in the "fairy tales," as he called them. My friend laughed heartily and chuckled, "Oh, you mean *that* Niatha^n! He was the *crazy* one! He wasn't God!" Still, the linguistic evidence leaves some room to explore this figure who was at once courageous, kind and ridiculous, totally primitive human, and still was reverently present at the moment of creation. Nih'a^{n}ca^n, in some accounts, gives the first man (and woman in some versions) the middle part of the earth to live in. It is he who, with the symbolic rock thrown into the primeval waters, determines the course of human destiny—that man is a being-in-the-world who must eventually die. Finally, he is recorded in some narratives as being taken up into heaven and called "Our Father."

When the old Indians venerated the other powers of nature and the heavenly bodies, it was with a mystic sense that they possessed life given from on high, a life that could somehow be communicated to mankind. Generally there was the idea that these powers were messengers of the Great Spirit. Hartley Burr Alexander narrates a dramatic account of how the Plumed Serpent rejoices at the new day of creation, and the ministering powers decree the beginning and end of that same creation, proclaiming a teleology as profound as any in the ancient world. Another creation myth, among the Minataree, has creation take place through the mediation of a man and a woman, here a man and his grandmother, who boil pots of water to provide life-giving rain. It is typical of the lack of imagination of so many Europeans who first heard such myths, that Prince Maximilian of Wied could see in such a story only crass "superstition." [9]

The various divine hierarchies can be typified by two examples in particular. One is the Pawnee tradition, the other the Arapaho, two tribes known for their broad and profound religious temperaments. The Pawnee place Tirawa, the Father, as Creator of all other beings, and below Him the Evening Star (female) and the Morning Star (male), who beget the first human being, a man. Below these are the Four World Quarters: the sacred personified winds of the northeast, the southeast, the southwest, and the northwest. Next are the three deities of the north, led by the North Star Chief, and below these Father Sun and Mother Moon, who give birth to the second human being, a woman. These humans are the progenitors of the race.

The Arapaho witness to a similar order, directing ritual prayers to Ichebeniatha[n], and next to the Four Old Men who care for the four sacred pipes and send the healing winds. Below them are the "Four Water-Dripping-Old-Men," now "canonized saints" who previously cared for the great Sacred Pipe and carried blessed water for the Sun Dance, having as their spiritual heirs today the four revered tribal religious elders. The Sun and Moon are deities, seen by some as two male figures in friendly competition, by

[9] David I. Bushnell, Jr., *Villages of the Algonquian, Siouan and Caddoan Tribes West of the Mississippi*, S. I., Vol. 77 (1922), p. 143.

others as man and wife. Nakox, the Morning Star, and He-thon-ha-tha, the Evening Star, were also divinities, and in Christian times the Morning Star has become the heavenly sign of the Christ: "Squint your eyes when you look at it in the early morning," I was told. "You'll see the cross right there in the sky."

As we shall discuss later, when Indians come together for a ceremonial smoking of the pipe, they use it to incense the Four Quarters, thus, by retracing the orderly shape of the universe, reminding themselves of their place as creatures in this sacred house called earth. Such a contemplative attitude even now, with so many tribal customs threatened with extinction or already gone forever, could well be reemphasized in the private and public lives of Christians searching for a sensitivity to the signs of nature and to human events. The swinging of the thurible at sacred ceremonies does not *have* to be outdated ritualism!

CREATION

The profession of creaturehood is man's first step back to God, and not merely a statement of curiosity about his origins. Creation myths grow up in human societies because they provide individual and collective answers to the questions of life and existence. There are numerous types of creation myths, the most sophisticated, to the biblical way of thinking, being the picture of a sovereign personal God tranquilly calling all things out of chaos. There are the colorful but violent theomachies of the Babylonians and the Iranians in which the way to creation is through warfare between opposing dual forces. Among some eastern Algonquian tribes we find myths of the war between light and darkness, good and evil. But the greater number of Amerindian myths point to the more gentle image (though also a morally neutral and relative one) of a concerned Providence giving man a *place* where he can *be* amid the waters of chaos. If one is tempted to infer here a Christian origin of such stories, he should ask himself why there is not a more clearly detailed image of the Creator than that offered. Rather, the accounts seem to be aboriginal by reason of their unique mode of expression, and yet in many aspects not unlike the stories in Genesis, though they do not emphasize the personal involvement of God in creation.

Most of these myths are of the "earth-diver" category, in which different animals are sent by primeval man or by the Creator to the bottom of the waters to find earth. Arapaho accounts tell of a man weeping because he has no place to put the Sacred Pipe. In response to his plaints many animals swim to his aid, and after a number have tried and failed, the turtle brings up earth from the floor of the sea. From this the man makes sod strips (celebrated annually by the making of the Sun Dance altar sods) out of which the floor of the earth is woven. From the same sod are made two figures of a man and a woman, the Creator breathes air into their nostrils, and the human race begins. There are similar versions among the Sioux, who make the muskrat the original earth-diver, and among the Cheyenne—in fact, among plains tribes in general.

There is a deeper, ascetic side to Indian origin myths, since all of them evince a pronounced dependency in man, a kind of poverty of spirit, which confirms Schleiermacher's notion that a "feeling of absolute dependence" is the basis of religion and the source of devotion. Certainly one who sees his origin as fashioned from the earth and breathed out from above will remain conscious both of a debt to the Creator and of the ground from which he is taken. Similarly, countless Indian stories of how man and beast were once one and of how man finally separated himself to become master of the buffalo, the birds, the bear, and the wolf, are touching accounts of how childhood naïveté gradually disappeared. But they are also reminders of humankind's dependence on those very elements it has mastered. Some of the most profoundly religious of all songs have been sung by Indian warriors and hunters, and by the aged as they came to realize their radical dependency:

> Father, have pity on me,
> Father, have pity on me,
> I die for thirst and there is nothing here to satisfy me!

> The old men say, only the earth endures.
> You have spoken truly, you have spoken well.

> Nothing lives long, only the earth and the mountains.

> Father, see us sitting here on the ground, poor and needy, surrounded by white people. . . .

> It is there that our hearts are set,
> In the expanse of the heavens.

> When you fear, in the dark before the dawn,
> take courage. . . .[10]

[10] In: Hartley Burr Alexander, *The World's Rim* (Lincoln, Neb.: University of Nebraska Press, 1969), p. 226; Frances Densmore, *Songs of the Teton Sioux,* S. I., Vol. 61 (1918), p. 357; Dee Brown, *Bury My Heart at Wounded Knee* (New York: Holt, Rinehart & Winston, 1971), p. 87; George A. Dorsey, *The Arapaho Sun Dance: The Ceremony of the Offerings Lodge* (Chicago: Field Columbian Museum, 1903), p. 148; Frances Densmore, *Pawnee Music,* S. I., Bulletin 93 (1929); the last excerpt is from an oral rendition of an Arapaho chant.

Hartley Burr Alexander once wrote that nowhere more than among these people is there recorded such a convincing belief that all of life is given to man as a period of petition and proof. The more tragic side of life on today's reservations is partly due to this sense of dependency, in which trust in Providence (the *use* nature of goods rather than their capitalistic value, and the absence of a competitive, acquisitive spirit in a world of competition) has left most Indians stripped of their old defenses and without adequate new ones.

ESCHATOLOGY

Attitudes toward life and death are influenced by the way in which one sees his creaturehood, or by the fact that he may or may not accept this world and himself as created at all. Many Indian tribal myths record how man's death-bound existence is determined from the moment of creation. In one story, a man in turtle moccasins casts a buffalo chip on the primeval waters, and as it floats atop the waves, he says, "As this buffalo chip floats, so shall man's life be." But the trickster has a far different idea, and casts a stone into the water; as it sinks he decrees, "*Thus* shall man's life be, for if men never die, soon we shall have no place to put them." Other tribes record that an old man casts the buffalo chip and his spouse casts the stone, with the words, "It is better for man to die, or else we will never have reason to feel pity for one another."

Living the precarious existence they did, Indians were bound to have a deep awareness of the proximity of the next world, to which they might pass quite suddenly through war, famine, or disease. Among the many songs reflecting on death are those of the very militant Sioux people, such as the brief war song that goes, "No one lives forever, old age is a curse." Again, a Pawnee song expounds on the value of dying bravely when young rather than living to a painful old age: "He comes. It hurts to use a cane. It becomes painful to pick it up." [11] And yet, the shunning of old age is only part of the tradition, for most Indian societies emphasize the dignity of the aged, partly because of their closeness to death and the next world, and rituals are oriented toward one's declining years.

Several early explorers recorded their shocked reactions to the unbridled grief and bloody self-mutilation they beheld at the funeral rites of many of the western tribes. One missionary priest, upon hearing the mourning wails of some members of one of the plains tribes, recalled "beseeching them to conclude these lugubrious accents"— and this overall air of condescension permeated most of the writings about Indians during the nineteenth century. There is no denying that, in many instances, the response to the death of a relative was bloody and uncontrolled, calling for the severing of finger joints and the gashing of one's own arms, legs, and torso. But those who may find this display disturbing could well examine much of the American death ritual of today, including the spectacle of places like Forest Lawn, where death is plastered over with a veneer of continued physical life.

Vine Deloria, Jr., writes about seeing a Roman Catholic priest trying to comfort a bereaved Indian woman by urging her not to weep for her dead son, who "surely was far better off now." Deloria wonders if the priest were not, rather, trying to reassure himself than to comfort the woman; this woman was fully aware that there is another

---

[11] Frances Densmore, *Pawnee Music,* S. I., Bulletin 93 (1929), p. 50.

life, but she was also admitting the sadness with which everyone faces human loss. What she needed was some release, an externalized acknowledgment of the pain of separation. Then she might indeed go about her business as before.

The value of honest sorrow always struck me whenever I attended a service for the dead in the home of an Indian family where the dead were waked either in the small house or in adjoining tipi. The keening of the women was as much a part of the ritual for the dead as the prayers we we recited verbally. The stereotype of the unemotional "wooden Indian" is one of the most horrendous distortions in all history.

An important addendum to any comments about death rituals and the attitude toward mourning is that here as in all cases we cannot generalize. Many writers record that tribes of their experience accustomed their members to endure the death of a loved one with quiet stoicism, however much they might grieve inwardly. It is also true of the tribes I have discussed above that there is today very little self-mutilation. The cutting of the hair as a sign of mourning is the bodily affliction most generally practiced. We shall discuss in a later chapter the custom of ritual comfort and encouragement given to bereaved family members, especially to children, in which a "life-must-go-on" philosophy is beautifully symbolized.

The general Indian belief in a world to come made it a simpler matter for them to acknowledge their creaturehood. Instances of pre-Christian burial rites indicate the strength of the mythology of death. Explorers and missionaries among the central and western tribes recount how the Indians professed the belief that the departed has gone on to a new life. In nearly all instances of Indian burial, whether earth burial or scaffold interment, various valuable implements were placed with the corpse. Accounts of plains Indian rites include descriptions of the shooting of a favorite horse or dog of the deceased. The heads and tails of these animals were nailed to the burial scaffold, or the bodies laid in the earth grave. Again, while one might validly question the economy of sacrificing good family beasts for a person's journey to the next world, one should not take these customs too literally. The burying of dead animals or the impaling of their heads and tails was an example of a mythical and symbolic consciousness of some kind of life beyond the grave that is *similar* to the one now experienced, somewhat like the Kingdom of Heaven pictured as a banquet or a wedding celebration. Such actions were effective symbols that would, it was hoped, sustain the departed as he or she "rode through the fair hunting grounds of the skies." Quite literally, it was a *viaticum* for the journey!

Indian death symbolism, like that of every other society, is hardly logical or coherent. One may read countless tales in Indian lore of the resuscitation of the dead and of reincarnation in new forms. Indians of the recent past used to consider abnormalities in new infants, whether physical disorders or strange conduct, to be signs that a child was an old person returned to earthly life. There are also stories of the passing alive from earth to heaven, such as the widespread myth of the woman who chased a porcupine up a tree into heaven and wound up as the wife of the sun or moon, later giving birth to twin hero-sons.

Theories about Indian belief in life after death are obscured by the fact that origin myths and "eschatological" myths are often so similar. What one hears today about passage from this world to the next might originally have been stories about how primitive peoples came from a lower world to this higher world. Or again, the myths may be a continuing description of a cycle of passages to ever new worlds. Thus, eschatology and origin myth are intimately related, as is the case in many religious traditions. In any case, most tribes believed in some version of life after death; believed, that is, in "the happy hunting grounds." Not all tribes seem to have believed in retribution, or separate places for good and evil, and even within believing groups there were apparently always agnostics. For example, some Arapaho did not allow for a "hell," because this acknowledgment would imply a judgment on the deceased by the living. However, others of the same tribe envisioned an "elsewhere," a consignment for certain serious sins such as suicide and other violently antisocial behavior. We find professed belief in retribution after death among the Saulteux (Chippewa) and the Sauk-Fox. The latter hold a traditional creed not unlike the Chinvat Bridge imagery of the ancient Zoroastrians of Persia. All the dead must cross a raging torrent on a narrow pole. If one's life had been honorable, the passage to the other shore would be a safe one; but if one had lived an evil life, he would fall into the river and be carried off to a place of misery. A similar Mandan myth shows the departed climbing a vine leading to heaven; if he had lead an evil life his passage was interrupted by a huge woman above him who would break the vine let down from paradise. If his life was a good one, the Lord of Life would bring him to happiness.

Many tribes of the southwest pictured the deceased wandering in a wasteland searching for rest and comfort, until he found a certain hill. After an arduous climb he would find a land of joy and peace on the other side. There is an Arapaho myth that, in addition to the soul's lingering near the camp for four days, the love of its relatives would also keep it from crossing over such a hill. Finally, however, the living would decide to let the soul go. Eventually, the combined love of those on the other side would draw all the living to the joys of that world—a rather striking version of a primitive social eschatology. Again, different Chippewa peoples believed that after death the spirit goes westward to where the sun sets, to the camping grounds of eternal happiness. Admission to these grounds required membership in the Mide wiwin lodge—a version of the doctrine of the elect.

This death mythology is not irrelevant to the various theologies of death which have been recently developed. Such theologians suggest that death is the ultimate determinant of the individual human "existence." Death is an ever-present "event" in the light of which one makes his life decisions—in fact, the one event that is always at least subconsciously present at every moment. The attempts of Indian mythology to give some meaning to the decision to accept death without despair indicate a similar understanding of its nature. The last description traditional Indians would give to death would be that it is merely "separation of body and soul."

One final comment on Indian eschatology: as I mentioned earlier, there are signs of a social view of eternity among many tribes, and this social bond determines how and when that end might take place. While many Indian tribes, especially among the Sioux, encourage a strong individualism both in life and in death, all of these tribes are thoroughly communitarian in their daily living. We find hints of this in the attitude toward death and the end of the world. Among the Arapaho we find later eschatological beliefs connected with the Sacred Pipe, the tribe's most revered possession. In addition to cherishing a ceremony of Covering the Pipe, the reward of which can be eternal life, the people believe that the evil deeds of men have led to a clogging of the Pipe, so that it can never again be smoked in this life. The Pipe has been gradually petrifying, and when it finally turns entirely to stone, the end will come. Christian Indians now connect this event with the Second Coming, just as they see the impressive dance of the Sunrise, held daily during the Offerings Lodge, to be a confession of hope that the Messiah will come to them as the Day-Star from on high (Luke 1:78), from the direction of the rising sun.

Beyond doubt such belief has some connection with the catastrophic Ghost Dance movement mentioned earlier, when many Indians considered the disappearance of the buffalo a sign of the end of the world, and their return the augur of a new world. It is heartening to know that the Wounded Knee massacre in 1890 did not entirely destroy this prophetic spirit. Many Indians today believe that with the coming together of the best elements of Christian, Indian, and other traditions, a genuine human fellowship can still be achieved. The book by Willoya and Brown, *Warriors of the Rainbow,* preaches this doctrine, as does the Brotherhood of Christian Unity, founded by Vine Deloria, Sr., father of the well-known Sioux author. Where such movements will terminate is a question not only for Indians but for the white churches as they respond to the needs of oppressed peoples.

COSMOLOGY

Cosmology, as the word itself indicates, is simply the study of an ordered world, or cosmos. In the modern era, traditional philosophical cosmology has given way to that of the positive sciences as interpretations of phenomena. And yet, mankind still searches for an explanation of the "mysterious universe" and the place of man within it. Thus, the purpose of cosmology is not now scientific or technological but existential and mythological. When man asks, "What is my world?" and "What does it say to me?" he is making a cosmological inquiry. American Indian lore is so impregnated with cosmological symbolism that it is impossible to cover every aspect of it in one book.

Hartley Burr Alexander, who was poet and philosopher as well as anthropologist, entitled one of his books *The World's Rim*. The title derives from a depiction of a plains Indian standing astride the earth, with arms outspread and held aloft, in communion with the powers and the winds that move about this rim. His skeletal frame, upright as opposed to that of four-legged creatures, is the measuring rod of the universe: his arms rotate to point in the four sacred directions, his head is to the heavens, and his feet planted on Mother Earth. We might even see here another version of the imagery of the Rabbis of the Hellenistic period who called Adam the image of universal man—his name in Hebrew meaning "man" and derived from *adamah*, "earth," and the Greek letters of his name being the first letters for east, west, north, and south.

Symbolically, this contemplative picture of man is Indian cosmology at its most typical, and describes the Indian's ordered world, a world created for him to enjoy and live in and to which he must be close companion. It is the symbol that most clearly explains why Indians have always had an intimate relationship with nature, whether in harmony or in terror. The agricultural tribes farther north and east drew their symbolism more from the imagery cele-

brated in the Delaware Big House ceremony, of which
Werner Mueller declared: "The basic religious attitude
which underlies all these rituals is the consciousness of living in a world (or a 'world house') full of living things."[12]
Each tribe, he explained, lives in a rounded and enclosed
cosmos and cosmology of its own—a reality so mysterious
that the experience of myth and visions becomes necessary
to ensure its perpetuation, mere dogma being inadequate
to the task. This "cosmic-house" concept is of great antiq-
uity, and is evident from one end of the North American
continent to the other.

In the recent film *Little Big Man* (one of the few among
even the more sensitive products of Hollywood to picture
Indian life perceptively), old Chief Lodgeskins of the Cheyenne laments to his young adopted white grandson that
the flaw in the white man is that he has lost the Center of
the universe. Consequently he can seek only to pillage and
destroy what he cannot truly feel at home with. No longer
do Whites stand firm within nature, but seek to tyrannize
it. Similarly, John G. Neihardt's *Black Elk Speaks* makes
this symbolism central to Black Elk's life. The holy man
describes how, as a boy of nine, he had a dream in which
he was carried to the Center of the world, above the nation's hoop, or circle-of-the-earth. He was shown the life
story of his people in elaborate imagery and dream language. From his commanding position he could see his
own vocation to save his people. Black Elk's eventual interpretation of the Center-of-the-world symbol is enlight-
ening, particularly in a "world come of age," a world of
demythologizing and of secularization. Whether the world

[12] Werner Mueller, "North America," in Walter Krickeberg, *et al., Pre-
Columbian American Religions* (New York: Holt, Rinehart & Winston, 1969), p. 168.

has truly come of age or not, one cannot help but be cut to the heart by the old man's simple words, "The Center of the universe is anywhere."

In song and narrative, the Center-image tells the Indians that the Creator has given them a sacred place. The Arapaho account tells how the Giver assigned this tribe to live in "the middle place." Their original name, Hinaneina, means simply "The People" as do many other original tribal names, each tribe seeing itself as chosen to hold fast to its own sacred space. Hence the great value placed on land and the devastation wrought among Indians when they found out that white men could not share it with them equitably. Even now, so I am told, Indians of the Wind River Reservation recognize four sacred shrines enclosing this restricted piece of land, as the place wherein the Creator will protect His people. The acceptance of sacred space, of a cosmos, is the doing of the will of God.[13]

We have already seen how the Four-Old-Men-of-the-Winds, how Sun, Moon, Earth, and Sky and the other powers are personified in Indian ritual prayers. Once more, the experience is cosmological. Personification of living things is certainly not to be equated with idolatry, but is, rather, the recognition that all things demand respect. The myths of how man came to rule the buffalo and other beasts are really empathetic stories symbolizing man's painful call to control nature, though never to lay it waste. They

[13] Today, when the Prairie Band Pottowatomi of Kansas seek to recover their land from the Missouri Province Jesuits, who no longer use it for their schools and missions, and then struggle to retain it over opposition from the Bureau of Indian Affairs, they are not overdramatizing when they appeal to their love for the land. Their reception back of the property from the Jesuits merited a combined Indian–Catholic religious rite and a great feast, with the exchange of symbolic gifts, because the sacredness of the land was being recognized.

describe also how much a part of existence suffering and death are, even though man must use his powers to over-come natural adversities. The Darwinian law of survival of the fittest could apply here, of course, except that in the modern, apparently sophisticated view of nature, man seems to have forgotten that his survival finally depends on his respect for the nature he transcends through his in-telligence. Even modern man lives in a cosmic house, how-ever far into space its ceiling may now protrude, and these Indian traditions witness to the basic human need to keep that house orderly.

Listening to Indians on reservations and in the cities de-scribe their own situations, one realizes how far from these traditions they themselves have been led. It might seem only nostalgic to seek to retrace old paths into a bygone age. However, in these same reservations and in urban In-dian groups one can see the old practices being followed. Ancient rites are used to worship the Creator (sometimes incorporated into traditional Christian services), ascetic practices are undertaken to open the sufferer to grace, nat-ural objects are employed as religious symbols, and above all, a pan-Indian movement is unifying the scattered tribes of the "diaspora." Families of many tribes, once hostile to one another, now camp around pow-wow grounds and the Sun Dance lodges during the summer season. Indians ma-rooned in large urban centers are gathering for ceremonies and feasts (often now timed to harmonize with their city jobs), for political and social action, into a supertribal as-sembly. Moreover, they are usually ready to include Whites here too, for the most basic thrust of Indian tradition is life in harmony.

Chapter Two

Celebration

THE RITUAL DIMENSION

Being as it were to be, long ago may I walk.
May it be happy before me.
May it be beautiful behind me.
May it be beautiful below me.
May it be beautiful above me.
May it be beautiful all around me.
In beauty it is finished, in beauty it is finished.

"Healing Song" from *The Navaho Night Chant*[1]

Awake, my soul!
Awake, O harp and lyre!
  I will awake the dawn!
I will give thanks to thee, O Lord among the peoples;
  I will sing praises to thee among the nations.
For thy steadfast love is great to the heavens,
  thy faithfulness to the clouds.
Be exalted, O God, above the heavens!
  Let thy glory be over all the earth!

PSALM 57:8–11

In the lyrics of the psalms, there is no doubt about the one
to whom all celebration is addressed, while in the chants
of the southwest Indians, celebrating the whole of nature's
healing power, we would be reading into the text to find

[1] Taken from Paul Radin, *The Story of the American Indian* (New York: Liveright Publishing Corporation, enlarged edition, 1944), p. 255.

there the One Lord as object of prayer. But in the songs of praise and exultation of Indian peoples there is certainly present the jubilant spirit of the psalmist. This frequent similarity to the spirit and imagery of the Old Testament is not surprising, for the physical environment, the basic needs, the tribal closeness are all comparable. The hymn with which I began this chapter is well known. Here it is quoted from a work of Paul Radin, but it is also cited in full by Hartley Burr Alexander and Margot Astrov, while N. Scott Momaday, the young Kiowa author, has used it as thematic for his Pulitzer Prize novel, *House Made of Dawn*. The natural flow of the cosmos into the ritual life of those who live close to it is celebrated in the entire chant.

Once again, the image is the Big House, the World Dwelling, the Great Lodge that we see rhapsodized here even as one might hear sung: "House made of Dawn . . . of evening light, of the Dark Cloud, of Male Rain, of Dark Mists, of Female Rain, of Pollen, of Grasshoppers and the zigzag Lightning"—and so on through the litany of those heavenly gifts to which the twelve nights of the Navajo festival sing their praise. Like the composers of the psalms, the unknown poet here praises the Powers with sacred smoke and asks for healing—of his feet, his legs, his body, his mind, his voice. He begs to go forth from all sickness with a cooling taste, no longer with soreness, with lively feelings; under the abundant dark clouds, with abundant showers, amid abundant plants, on the trail of pollen may he walk—that it may be finished in beauty.

On one occasion several summers ago, I was entertaining a visitor at an Indian reservation in Wyoming. We drove to the foothills of the Wind River Mountains, then began winding up the switchback road. As we reached an elevation of about two thousand feet above the vast basin, my

visitor remarked, "I think I have an idea why Indians do
not take easily to white ways." When a person finds himself perched atop the world's rim, he does feel the technological society slipping rapidly from his consciousness. He
probably becomes a romantic, for the time at least. And
this quality of romanticism, moderated by a balancing re-
alism, is what Indians most often are by temperament—a
fact with its tragic shading as well. But for now, we shall
try to learn what this living in the World House meant to
the first dwellers in North America, and what it still does
mean to them as they sit and look across the miles of sage
and valleys to the mountains and the sunset. There are similar experiences in other parts of the country, certainly, but
here it becomes easy to understand why the Indians of the
high plains considered the sunset and sunrise to be *the*
hours of prayer. It is significant that, when an Arapaho
greets someone with "ēthētē nà kusëch"—Good morning—
he uses a word, *ēthētē,* that means both "beautiful" and
"good." Apparently in the Navajo tongue, beauty means
happiness as well.

The traditional Indian lived not in chronological but in
cosmic time, and in sacred space rather than in the physical
dimensions marked off by cartography. Cosmic time is not
clocked; it is world time, measuring periods of importance,
like the time of a sun dance, of a hunt, or of a "moon,"
rather than the details of a daily schedule. Time in this
sense is at the root of what many Indians mean when they
say jokingly, "It will begin at nine *Indian* time." That is,
it begins when we all get there—except when meeting the
sunrise or the sunset is involved. The sentence is a humorous one, but it has very serious traditional groundings. The
equivalent Greek word, used in the New Testament, might
be *kairos*—a fitting, chosen time, influenced and chosen by

eternity, by God. Sacred space is the space of the Four Winds, the ground on which one stands to greet the sun and to pray, to experience the blessings of creation. Jacob experienced it in Genesis 28:17, when he blurted out after his vision, "How awesome is this place!" Sacred space is represented by the tribal camp circle, which in former times was held together by its own special religious rites and obligations. The tribal circle was the circle of the earth, and the tribe, or clan, encamped around the Center of the universe.

Closely related to this cosmic viewpoint is what traditional theology would call a deeply "sacramental" outlook on creation. Everything is *given* to man for use and should be offered to the Creator. Some Indian "excesses," as we might call them, such as minor mutilations and severe fasting, are based on the notion that to give back something of the body is the highest form of devotion. The fact that nearly all traditional Indian rituals are in surroundings built directly from what the land offers, and employ material taken directly from nature, is related to this same notion that all creation is a manifestation of the Spirit.

RITUAL AS SACRAMENT
OF CREATION

No one witnessing the impressive sunrise prayer-dance of the Arapaho Offerings Lodge can escape feeling that here is liturgy from the cosmos itself. Indian ritual is in every way a cosmological sacrament, and it is as such that we must describe and discuss it here. It is, of course, difficult for Whites to avoid reading a conscious monotheism into Indian prayers, with the resultant error that one tends to call Indian rites "worship" instead of "communion" with the Powers. But taking worship in the broad sense of reverential service, we can use the term with assurance.

Authorities like Radin and John Collier point out that the ceremony called the Sun Dance, based on the Sioux description, "dance-facing-the-sun," is actually of rather late origin (probably late eighteenth century) and of a highly eclectic nature. That is, as the various plains tribes saw their "Center" gradually disintegrating because of increasing nomadism and white intrusion, they set out to rediscover that Center as best they could. Thus, the Sun Dance is an amalgam; it contains many ancient symbols and practices, but all as parts of a new setting. Similarly, many details of the Sun Dance differ from tribe to tribe, from Sioux to Arapaho to Cheyenne to Blackfoot to Shoshone. But among all these groups there are common elements.

There is the origin of the dance in a vow made by one person either in petition or in thanksgiving. For example, the Arapaho reception of the Sun Dance for their own involved a young mother and her baby who somehow managed to escape a white assault on their camp. As she hid in fear in the willows by a riverbank, she made a vow to undertake a great sacrifice if she and her child would be spared. It so happened that they were spared and the story goes that the woman's brother then pledged to erect the Offerings Lodge and perform the ordeal of the dance.

At a given day in summer there is then the assembling of the tribe around a center—the calling-together of the scattered people in the name of the Creator, not basically different from the purpose of the prayer for unity in the ancient Christian *Didache*. There follow (while many secret preparatory lodge rites go on) the scouting and cere-

monial killing of a straight young tree, and its trimming
and raising, again at the center of the camp. With this the
lodge-maker begins to fulfill his vow and is joined by
other men who are to undergo the ordeal, and by women
and musicians who assist them.

As we noted earlier, the Sun Dance has not perished, as
so many white scholars thought it would. It has undergone
certain adaptations, and yet remains astonishingly the
same, at least as far as I could detect by comparing Dorsey's notes of 1903 with my own personal experiences in
1970, 1972, and 1973. Perhaps the best way to convey an
understanding of this rite will be to describe an actual
dance.

Let us imagine a dry, clear, 95-degree Monday afternoon
in mid-July as one enters a large campground of perhaps
a hundred acres, containing mostly dry, tough prairie
grass, clumps of sagebrush, and a few small trees. Already
some tents have been pitched, and tribal leaders are at
work, unhurriedly setting up a large tipi about fifteen feet
in diameter and a Sweat Lodge nearby. The modern touch
is also present as a public-address booth is being organized
alongside the inner circle. There is no particular air of
worship discernible, only scattered conversation and occasional glimpses of the religious director as he moves deliberately about the tipi, and to and from his own lodgings
nearby. What is beginning to occur inside this Rabbit
Lodge, as the tipi is called, is not revealed to spectators, but
one can gather that the many rites of preparation are now
taking place. Although it is known that Indian tribes from
their ancient prehistory have been aware that man descends
—or ascends—from the animal world; and although it is
common knowledge that tribal clans, or moieties, where
they existed, took their names from some beast of the ani-

mal kingdom, it is never made clear exactly why the Arapaho call this ceremony after the rabbit.

It is likely that this small lodge represents the sacred mountain where the originator of the Sun Dance learned his sacred duties. So, one might imagine that the men and women inside, instructing and learning, smoking ceremonially, feasting and then fasting for three days, are symbolically returning to the origin of their worship. There are no scrolls or stone tablets here, for the Arapaho tradition is entirely oral, but the memory of their own "Sinai" is in the minds of those who truly understand the ceremony.

As one returns on the Tuesday and Wednesday following, he will see nothing greatly different, except that the number of tents, cars, and trailers surrounding the center is increasing, so that the entire acreage is gradually being worn down to dust and brown grass. Many of the men gather around the public-address booth to sit quietly, joke, and observe what little activity there is. The busiest persons visible are the women who, at certain intervals, must prepare a large feast for the Lodge-Pledger, the holy man, and other participants, prior to and at the end of their fast from food and water.

On Wednesday evening, the Sweat Lodge has been removed, but the Rabbit Tipi remains, and the Lodge-Pledger is resting inside on the final night of his fast. With him are his family, the holy man, and the drummers. If one is invited into the tipi he will enter a dimly lit sanctuary where a fire burns and sends shadows darting about the silent figures of the lodge. The drummers will be beating out a 4/4 beat and singing a song that seems to be more a chant than actual words. As one crosses his legs and sits silently, it becomes increasingly easy to be totally involved in the shadows and the drums. If one can imagine that the very physical sounds and movements heard and seen are the traditional Indian form of discourse with the supernatural, one may find it possible to meditate without words, joining into the hypnotic beat of the song.

The following day brings the raising of the lodge pole. If one reads accounts of the elaborate ceremony of the felling of the sacred tree, he will have a more or less complete picture of the tradition of the hunt and of the rites immediately preparatory to the erection of the Offerings Lodge —the true name of the Arapaho version of the Sun Dance. At an equivalent ceremony, the Shoshone still go through the old custom of the sham battle and slaying of the tree, with the traditional "counting coup" (touching it with a stick or bow). No doubt the tree symbolizes, at the time of capture, the tribes' common enemies, until it later becomes the benevolent symbol within the lodge, converted into the Center.

The pole by now has been painted with black and red circles—the Arapaho colors, as some say, representing the sun's heat and night's quiet, or the red of blood-courage and the black of joy. Colored cloth votive offerings have been tied to the pole near the fork at the top, as well as to the other supporting roof-poles still lying on the ground, and in the fork of the pole is the sacred bundle containing such things as sweet sage, the thunderbird's nest, and other sacred objects. As time comes, late in the afternoon, to raise the pole, there seems to be no discrimination about who might help raise it. At the direction of a chief of operations, the crew of men raises the treetrunk with grunts and shouts, until it falls into place. The older tradition of three false lifts no longer seems to be observed. The pole has become once again the Tree of Life and rests in the navel of the earth. The Center is again established.

It remains for twelve smaller poles, already standing around the center, to be connected to form sides and a quasi-roof. Further poles are tied horizontally from one of these to the other to complete a circle some seventy-five feet in diameter. Then another twelve poles, the ones filled with votive-scarves, are raised through the forks of the small poles crossed over the horizontal bars, to come to rest in the larger fork of the Center pole, and all are fastened in place. A carnival atmosphere now prevails, and trucks carrying great loads of leafy willow branches drive up. Everyone responds to the call for help in the lodge-raising, and helps assemble the brush tightly around the lodge, to create a closed area open only to the east. Following this, the holy man of the tribe leads a line of young men into the new lodge to dance a quiet round dance called the Fox Dance—apparently intended to introduce younger men and boys to the sacred customs.

Further preparations of the early evening now include the building of an altar to the west of the pole. The altar is on the ground, and consists of a buffalo skull, painted with red and black dots, with sprigs of sage stuck into its empty eye-sockets. In front of it a small pit about six inches deep is dug and freshly cut sods are laid evenly into it, symbolic of the strips of earth from which the first man, or the Creator himself, fashioned the dwelling-place for mankind. This is further symbolic, for the lodge itself now becomes the center of the universe and man's true home, situated within the horizon, which is represented by the wider camp circle whose boundaries the Four Old Men now hold firm. At some time here also, the wooden strip for the Sacred Wheel—*hŏ hŏti*—is taken from the holy man's bag and bound once more into a hoop, which is said to represent both the nation and a small snake that bodes good tidings for the tribe. The wheel is decorated with eagle feathers, to be given over into the possession of the Lodge-Pledger who has sponsored, or as Arapaho say, "put up" the dance.

An additional and very important rite that one would witness if he were present the afternoon before the erection of the lodge is the Pledger's begging tour. In this ceremony, the principal vovant, wrapped in a buffalo robe, walks slowly around the camp circle—at least a mile in circumference—while a wagon or truck follows him, into which all present are asked to put food and provisions to allay expenses for the ceremony. The ceremony also symbolizes the tremendous importance of food to a people for whom the danger of famine was never far away.

Toward midnight, "ritual time," the beginning of the three-day event is at hand, and preparations are under way. The dancers, having feasted that evening, now begin their fast from food and water, and each one, with the help of his "grandfather"—a sponsor who has himself danced in the ceremony—is painted in white clay all over his body for this first rite. He wears the decorated apron over a loincloth or shorts, and the revered eagle-bone whistle hangs about his neck. Each grandfather embraces his grandson and whispers to him some final instructions. Then the leaders begin a staccato shaking of bone rattles and a soft *ay-ya* chant, while the men move in alternate quarter-circles about the lodge, increasing their movements enough to vary their individual positions. They stop and raise one or both arms to each world corner respectively, while blowing on their whistles. When these alternating circles have been completed, the participants have saluted all of the Four Old Men.

The drummers begin their beat and the participants now become sacred, as the remaining elements of the old "dancing-in" rite are completed. They bounce slowly up and down, moving the upper legs and torso vertically, keeping time on their whistles. This is the inaugural ceremony about the Tree of Life, where they will fast, dance, sing, and cry for three days, unapproached by anyone except their grandfathers and other assistants.

The following is a description of a typical Offerings Lodge day, Friday through Sunday. Before sunrise each morning, the grandfathers are awakend by the leaders (the Pipe-Keeper or the Director, who is, currently at least, the chief tribal medicine man), and they in turn awaken their charges, who are sleeping on beds of reeds arranged about the central and western edges of the lodge, bundled up in blankets against the chill night. As one watches in the predawn, he will see the men in their full garb, with only their paintings varied. On the feet are moccasins, and from the waist down is the ceremonial apron brightly decorated with a variety of Indian, patriotic American, and Christian symbols. Nothing is worn on the upper torso except the whistle and perhaps a scapular or rosary or religious medal—a witness to grassroots syncretism. On succeeding days, one will observe changes of painting, on a body-paint background of yellow, red, or white, and black or red markings in patterns handed down through generations. By the end of the second day, the men also wear sage bunches tucked into their waists and wristbands, and a crown of sage on their heads. Eagle tufts are fastened to the crowns and to the whistles.

As the men form a horseshoe facing the Sacred East, the

drummers take their places as one of the lead assistants shouts out instructions in Arapaho. The Sacred Pipe arrives in procession on the second morning. The spectators are ordered to form ranks along the entrance so that no one stands between the lodge-opening and the sun. An old man stations himself slightly to the south of the entrance outside. The drums begin the same 4/4 beat accompanied by chanting, while the dancers begin their stationary dance, and blow time on their whistles, alternately raising and lowering their arms to the sun as it begins to rise over the distant horizon. The Lodge-Pledger dances and waves the Sacred Wheel aloft and downward, first in his left hand and then in his right, again in the direction of the sun. The vigil has again been kept, and the sun begins to appear in the sky, flooding the lodge with a new dawn. As the sun arrives full in the sky, the music ceases, and the old man shouts further instructions.

Later in the day one may witness an example of the famous Arapaho "giveaway." People of this tribe are known for their elaborate gifting on special occasions, including the self-divesting (like the Potlatch of the far northwest) of the family at the death of a close relation, and even for no special reason, except to show friendship. During this ceremony, many families of the dancers, out of gratitude to God as well as to win favors from Him, and in hospitality to guests from other tribes, announce valuable gifts— blankets, utensils, clothing—for special persons they have selected. Recipients will often show public gratitude by dancing briefly and chanting a prayer of thanks, or, in the case of the women, singing a shrill yodel-like song of appreciation.

In the late afternoon, the dancers will be bathed, each grandfather ceremonially dipping sweet sage into a bucket of cool water and touching his grandson's body with it. The dancer finishes cleaning off the old paint, using the sage as a washcloth, and concludes by pouring the remaining water over his head, being careful to drink nothing. If one watches carefully, he will observe the grandfather encouraging the tiring man and perhaps even fanning him in the afternoon heat. Many women weep publicly for the dancers in this ordeal.

Formerly among the Arapaho, before the turn of the century, and often still today among the Sioux, the afternoon of the third day is the time of the torture. Here the dancer would be suspended from the pole by a rawhide thong skewered into his pectoral muscles, or would have a buffalo skull trailing from a thong embedded in his shoulder blades, until the flesh tore away. Most tribes have ceased the practice, partly because the government frowns on it, but also because (according to Dorsey) it was originally a strengthening for battle, and battles today are fought more in the spirit and mind than in the body. But the torture has not entirely vanished among the Sioux, who have successfully defied official displeasure; even many Christian Indians simply say, "Didn't Jesus suffer worse for us? This is a way to do something for Him." Whatever the theology here, the personal asceticism involved is awesome.

When one returns on the final evening, he will observe that the Sacred Pipe—Saetcha^n—installed since the second morning on a tripod near the center, has been covered with quilt offerings. These gifts are draped over the bundle, after which the devotee places his or her forehead on the bundle and prays silently to the Creator and the Powers for the tribe, all of which are somehow gathered up symbolically in the Sacred Pipe. The offerings, having been so consecrated, are later distributed to elderly people in need.

As the dancers and chanters—men and women—cease their drumming early in the evening, the western end of the lodge will be ripped away. The onlookers, who may number as many as two thousand, then line up in ranks on either side of the lodge, leading out toward the mountains where the sun is to set and the evening star will appear. The Sacred Pipe is carried out of the eastern entrance in procession, a woman bearing it on her back, so that later it can be "walked" home ("walking" the Pipe is mandatory) to the Keeper's house some three miles away over the hills. The final dance has been called "Gambling against the Sun"—pitting one's last ounce of strength against the last bit of sacred time, measured clockwise as about a half hour. To finish this without flagging is to have completed the vow most devotedly. As the sun drops behind the mountains, the music ceases and families run to embrace fathers, husbands, and brothers who have finished the rite, offering them the traditional drink of cherry-water as a purgative. Each dancer then deposits his sagebrush crown atop the woven branches of the sod altar, from which the buffalo skull has been removed, and with this final silent offering, departs with his family to the feast.

I have chosen to describe the ceremonies of the Arapaho Sun Dance, because it is a synthesis of nearly all the ancient symbols of the plains tribes with newer historical elements. Had one gone in spirit to the neighboring Shoshone Sun Dance, he would have seen similar surroundings but a more sprightly two-step type dance and frequent acts of "charging the pole" by dancers wearing no paint but more elaborate aprons. In general, among the Shoshone one would have seen a more carnival-like, less solemn celebration.

Such a festival as the Sun Dance might well become an inspiration for fragmented white Christian congregations. A ceremony of this type could serve to exemplify a religio-social gathering, in which religious and social rites are joined with skillful imagination. The problem here is, of course, the time-span needed to carry out such festivities: a full week taken off for celebration is largely a fossil in most of American life, except in very closely knit ethnic communities. Perhaps three or four weekends could be employed to weave together religious rites, instruction by qualified persons, games, dining, and some form of social concern fitted to the parish situation. The Sun Dance did succeed in holding tribes together amid almost cataclysmic change, and helped them to face it with greater courage and adaptability. The analogy to contemporary white America's own crumbling social order is not a forced one, and the possibilities here are worth examining.

Any Christian familiar with the spirit of St. Francis of Assisi will have no trouble empathizing with Indian allusions to Sun, Moon, Fire, and Water as brothers, sisters, and intimate friends. What Francis apparently experienced is remarkably like the goal of Indian prayer and worship, expressed so typically by the various calumet or pipe ceremonies. In these rites, the blowing of smoke to the Four Corners, to the Middle Point, to Heaven, and to Earth illustrates the ritual sense of oneness with the cosmos, and is thus the most typical Indian ceremony for establishing peace.

We have already discussed the concept of oneness with God, and we shall take up later the ways to union with one's true self and with the neighbor. But the relationship to the universe seems to be the fundamental experience, and can be found in Amerindian rites throughout North

America. This is not to say that such rituals were always and in every way what Whites or even modern Indians would accept as true worship today. There was human sacrifice (though known only in one case—the Pawnee Morning Star—north of the Rio Grande), vengeful black magic, occasional cannibalism and torture of enemies, not unlike rites of other ancient societies. But gradual evolution, sometimes helped by Christianity and sometimes opposed by it, has underlined the importance of oneness with nature. Analogous to the Sun Dance of the plains Indians are the various agricultural festivals in the eastern and southwestern United States, for example, the different Green Corn festivals. We have already referred to the annual assembly of the Florida Seminole to pray for the sustenance and welfare of the tribe, as well as to fast, to test powers of endurance by ritual flesh-scratching, to dance together, and to drink the "black drink" that purges the inner person. This was a time, as I shall explain, when tribal justice was also carried out, and we see it so practiced among the Five Civilized Tribes and many others at time of festival. Ruth Underhill has observed how careful many of the hunting tribes were to offer their apologies to the creatures on whom they preyed, and even more to enact whole rituals imitating the animals they slaughtered.[2]

All tribes were conscious of the earth as a mother, as *their* mother, and thus the prophet of the northwest, Smohalla, even refused to plow the ground, lest he rend his mother's breast. The fertility rituals among the tribes of the southwest, especially the Pueblo, were not merely the occasion of asking for rain and a good crop. They were

[2] Ruth M. Underhill, *Red Man's Religion* (Chicago: University of Chicago Press, 1965), pp. 116ff.

times of healing and of psychic restoration for which the people counted on the earth's powers of fecundity.

It is striking how this sense of supernatural power was revered, especially in the person of a woman. Perhaps many liberated women would be horrified at the custom of having a menstruating woman live in a separate wigwam, as the central Algonquian did, or of a young Navajo woman in her period doing no work and living in ritual idleness in a ceremonial house. That proven virginity should once have been a requirement for performing certain rituals (now apparently open to married women), such as the cutting of the Arapaho Sun Dance pole, would now be taken as primitive "taboo" or "magicalism." Maybe we are correct in having gotten "beyond" such views, but, as with most primitive rites, there is a lesson to be learned. The menstruating woman is evidently a vessel of the power to give new life, and in this sense no doubt men felt inferior to her, even fearing that her presence would curse their killing expeditions on hunt and warpath.

The young virgin had special powers because she was innocent, and all youngsters were sent off on wilderness fasts to seek visions prior to puberty, after which they were no longer innocent enough to have pure visions. I mention this attitude because of the tendency to be taken aback by the rare but periodic ritual license formerly allowed during the Sun Dance ceremonies, or by certain practices of sexual imagery in the ceremonies of the Papago of Arizona. We frequently have forgotten the extreme precaution taken in earlier periods of Indian history with regard to chastity and courtship. Indian society in most instances was not one of sexual promiscuity.

Here it may be to the point to inquire into the depth of

contemporary Western man's oneness with created life, and his sensitivity to natural forces, stripped by technology of all aura of mystery. Similarly, one might gain from a deeper knowledge of the work of medicine men and shamans, who negotiate with the Powers and try to direct them to healing activity. Many are the Indian witnesses who claim cures worked by their Indian doctors after white medicine had apparently failed. I have listened in detail to such accounts. Though we should not here commit the primitivist fallacy of rejecting modern scientific progress, neither can we dismiss the holistic views of psychosomatic medicine and "healing of the spirit" that might occur in such a milieu.

SONG AND DANCE

Several years ago after a service on Sunday at the opening of an Indian pow-wow, I noticed a middle-aged couple, their children and relations walking solemnly to the outer circle of the grounds. With the parents at the head of the procession, the family began a slow round dance to the one-two beat of the drum. The father of the family carried a photograph of a woman, holding it against his chest, face outward. I realized soon that they were doing a round dance for the dead, an ancient requiem prayer in motion, for the woman's dead mother. In such a rite, it becomes evident how essential the dance is to Indian worship and how moving an experience religious dancing can be. Students of Indian culture have marveled at the depth to which dancing has penetrated the Indian soul, not as entertainment, although this too is important, but first of all as a religious experience. Religious origins, too, are probably the inspiration for the Cherokee "Stomp Dance." In this ceremony a young man leads a chorus of other young people about the dance circle, with music supplied not by drums but by antiphonal chanting and the stomping of the girls, who wear heavy tortoise-shell rattles strapped to their legs. It is possible that the religious symbolism of the turtle lent power to this dance, since turtles are sacred to many tribes.

Countless tribal and intertribal myths tell of man's ongoing dialogue—often violent—with the eagle or thunderbird, with beasts of prey like the wolf or bear or cougar, and with the smaller beasts like the rabbit, skunk, porcupine, and field mouse. William Fenton's lengthy research into and description of the Eagle Dance among the tribes of the Iroquois Confederacy describes for us a ritual that entails not only the typical integration of the social and the religious, but celebrates man's union with nature as well. The dancers imitate the movements of the great bird, even to the graceful act of picking up corn kernels or pennies with the teeth while balanced on one leg. This dance in some form is widespread even into the southwest, and is done today in a less ceremonial form by the Arapaho. Dances imitating other birds and beasts are common, but the most beautiful is the dance that mimics the eagle in its ascending and descending flight. Some scholars believe that even the Sun Dance is an imitation of the angry wounded buffalo bull.

These dances do as a matter of fact provide entertainment, and today many of them are performed for that purpose, but they signify much more in their origin: the union between earth and heaven and all levels of life. For example, there is the famous story that has filtered down to the Iroquois from tribes farther west about the young warrior who was kidnaped by the great Dew Eagle and carried to her nest in the Rockies where she initiated him into the world of the great birds of prey. He was finally returned by this bird (who is believed to be a special messenger of the Creator) to his own tribe, to whom he relates his story of the other world. What Fenton calls the "touchstone of Iroquois religion" can probably characterize, other things being equal, Indian religious rites and myths in general:

> The touchstone of Iroquois religion is this whole concept of augmented reverence progressing through the various stations of the pantheon, from the earth upward to the sky world, as opposed to fear and dread of malefic beings on and beneath the earth.[3]

The predance invocation of the Dew Eagle becomes an all-encompassing prayer as the dancers are told to meditate on all the messengers of the Creator, finally arriving at the One Creator himself. Fenton quotes the tobacco-burning invocation:

> Now you will partake of tobacco, you who are wheeling in flight at the elevation the clouds are scudding, you who are of the mists—the Dew Eagles.
> Now the smoke is rising from the real tobacco and through it you cloud dwellers shall hear.
> Rightly our ruler ordained as he intended (or said), "I will create mankind on the earth, that there shall travel to and fro human beings to whom, no matter where they are, aid shall come from time to time."

[3] William N. Fenton, *The Iroquois Eagle Dance, an Offshoot of the Calumet Dance*, S. I., Bulletin 156 (1953), p. 92.

And they tobacco shall partake, they whom he created, the wild animals; and they (humans) shall continue to derive benefit from a bond of friendship between themselves and the game animals.[4]

Among the arts of supernatural communication we can also place singing and instrumental music. Only at times are there words to an Indian song, and these are generally very brief; often the songs are mere syllabic chants. The real source of power and communication with nature derives from the total absorption of the singer in his or her rhythm and melody, much as the communication that is evident among great jazz musicians goes back to the religious roots of their music. One observes a very similar spirit among Indian singers. Anyone who has sat inside the ceremonial tipi of the Rabbit Lodge late at night realizes that the ceaseless pounding and high-pitched singing are anything but mere entertainment.

Frances Densmore tells us that Indians believe in an experiential connection between song and the supernatural—a communication once more of power.[5] This is borne out by the fact that Indians traditionally sang on every momentous occasion, as well as on ordinary ones. At the birth of a child they sang, and at the moments celebrating significant growth. They sang at burials and in other times of sadness, and at the times of peace-making and at the return of hunting and war parties. It is recorded, too, that white army personnel were shocked and then condescendingly derisive at the shrill death songs of the rebel Santee

[4] *Ibid.,* p. 59.
[5] Frances Densmore, "Technique in the Music of the American Indian," S. I., Bulletin 151 (1953), No. 36, pp. 213–216.

Sioux warriors as they mounted the gallows and chanted to the Powers of heaven they were soon to join.

RITES OF PLAY AND HUMOR

Occasionally, in conversations with older Indian people, I will bring up the matter of the many traditional stories, myths, and legends in their history. These stories are generally loosely grouped under the headings of Mythical Instruction, Moral Exhortation, and Entertainment. Generally the very mention of these stories will draw a chuckle of glee, because it is difficult to separate one kind of story from the other. For example, the role of the trickster runs through everything from creator to culture-hero to simple buffoon. Many of the ridiculous situations he and other characters get themselves into point to some kind of moral flaw, usually marital infidelity, deceit, murderous intent, or incest. Anthropologists have never managed to unravel this tangled web, but one possible solution may lie in the ritual nature of story-telling. One can imagine a young person, wanting to be instructed in the traditions of the tribe, "putting up" a feast for his elders (the usual way to get oral tradition in motion), and the whole group seated around a fire following the masterful narration of tales. Or, as some of the myths themselves tell us, the neophyte had to pass through several successive nights of listening in order to learn the whole tribal history. Certainly a good instructor knew when to combine mirth and seriousness, solemnity and comic relief. Not even religion, the Indians believe, should be idolized and made immune to humor, for it too is human.

Most Indian people are blessed with wit and humor, and enjoy baiting others and being baited. Indeed, all religious traditions allow a place for humor and clowning. Christianity had its Feast of Fools, Judaism its Purim holiday, Hinduism its playful Krishna, and Taoism its subtle puzzles. It is in this same spirit that one can understand the ritualized fun in the rubrics for intermoiety ridicule in the Iroquois Eagle Dance. Fenton refers to this rite as a natural vehicle for personality expression.[6] In addition, since the dance is often held to cure a sick person, the joking and insults are intended to help him forget the pain and suffering.

Many Indian religious festivals are accompanied by games. These may not necessarily be what we would call "religious experiences," but are, rather, comparable to what takes place at any large family picnic. And yet among the Indians it was taken for granted that the game belonged to the festival, or often that it of itself had a religious or moral value. Black Elk recounts a ritual ballgame played among the Sioux, Tapa Wanka Yap ("The Throwing of the Ball"), which the holy man calls sacred because it represents, by the very difficulty of catching the ball, the course of human life and the life of the tribe:

> At this sad time today among our people, we are scrambling for the ball, and some are not even trying to catch it, which makes me cry when I think of it. But soon I know it will be caught, for the end is rapidly approaching, and then it will be returned to the center, and our people will be with it.[7]

[6] Fenton, *op. cit.,* p. 38. On banter as part of the cure of the sick, see p. 72.

[7] Black Elk (with Joseph Epes Brown), *The Sacred Pipe* (Norman: University of Oklahoma Press, 1970), p. 138.

The southeastern tribes played a ballgame in connection with the Green Corn festivals. It consisted of two teams, boys against girls generally, in which a flat board was fastened to a pole some twenty feet high. The whole effort of the game was to get the ball (girls using lacrosse-type rackets and boys their bare hands) and hurl it against the elevated board. Capron remarks that tribal elders saw the roughhouse connected with this game as one of the preliminaries to courtship. Watching modern Cherokee young people demonstrate this game lets the viewer see how this ritualized mingling would prove an outlet for an otherwise strictly governed sexual milieu where even ordinary social contact would be severely restricted.

The most moving of all explanations for the mingling of humor and religion may be that of Black Elk, whose prophetic dream fulfillment may be coming at long last in the form of the inspiration his works give to people of all races. Among the plains Indians there were occasional examples of young men who because of a bizarre vision or some personal aberration went around doing everything backward—riding horses face-to-rear, washing in sand and mud, answering No when they meant Yes, and so on. The Oglala Sioux called them *heyoka* ("crazy") and a whole ceremony grew up around the idea. The Arapaho word for "crazy" is a similar sounding *ha hawkan,* and was a name formerly given to holy men on occasion, much like Dostoevsky's holy "idiot," or St. Francis, the *idiota* of Assisi. In the *heyoka* ceremony men and boys engaged in general tomfoolery, with heads half-shaved, horses half-painted, bows too long to use and unstrung, arrows more curved than the bows. And why such clowning as a religious act? Black Elk speaks his wisdom:

You have noticed that the truth comes into the world with two faces. One is sad with suffering, and the other laughs; but it is the same face, laughing or weeping. When people are already in despair, maybe the laughing face is better for them; and when they feel too good and are too sure of being safe, maybe the weeping face is better for them to see. And so I think that is what the heyoka ceremony is for.[8]

THE RITUAL OF THE LIFE CYCLE

I have reserved this discussion for the end of this chapter because of its profound significance, particularly for the white Christian, who might well ask himself how his own tradition deals with the "life story." Or, does life simply pass the Christian by without commentary, save for a birthday or an anniversary? Does the mystery that is called life demand to be symbolized and mythologized—in sum, integrated into a whole? The Indians have always believed that it does, and their tradition makes a natural context for the celebration of traditional Christian rites of initiation and human growth.

Hartley Burr Alexander has detailed an excellent account of the Four-Hills-of-Life mythology as practiced among the Siouan Omaha Indians. But the tradition seems to be wide-spread. My own understanding of it was enhanced by listening to an Arapaho version, which calls it "The Four Buttes." The picture of the butte makes the imagery more striking: man approaches four high, flat-topped, natural hills in order—infancy and childhood, youth, middle life, and old age—while the other world waits beyond the final descent. A butte has steep rocky sides and is never easy to ascend; once scaled, it affords a stretch of flat space for walking, and a panorama of the world. Descent is again arduous, but one knows that he must go down, and begin the next climb. It is a contemplative's vision of life and death, and Arapaho tradition even tells several myths of the man-animal hero White Owl, whose special office it is to guard the passage along the road of the Four Hills.

Nearly every tribe has rituals that begin with prenatal care. Immediately following birth, the umbilical cord was dried and placed in a bag, to be left hanging on the child's cradle, then carried in his belt, and finally to go with him back into Mother Earth's bosom. After the birth of the child, the cradle was incensed at its four corners with cedar smoke, and the child was blessed and prayed over. The Omaha priests used to perform a dedication ceremony and give the child its name. At the naming ceremony among the Arapaho, the infant was passed from one relative to the other as all sat in a circle on the floor, while each prayed for the child's coming life-course. Recent Christian baptisms among these people have often been accompanied by the traditional naming ceremony, as the child received names representing two ancient traditions.

It would demand too much space to detail all the examples of ritual activity that assisted the infant into life and along its first climb toward youth. Essential to that ascent were various occasions in which the child could learn by using the full power of its imagination. It was a natural custom that long preceded theorists like Schleiermacher, who called for the religious development of children not to stifle the imagination by premature exercise of conceptual and abstract teachings. Thus, the child could look forward, at the latest around the age of four or five, to an ear-piercing ceremony, perhaps at a festival like the Sun Dance. If he should be ill, he would be prayed over by the men undergoing the ordeal. He might even enjoy several naming occasions for special reasons in the course of his young life. The loss of the first tooth was often a special event among Indians.

Nearly all Indian children were taught to listen respectfully to old people, who could teach them the wisdom of life and good conduct. Ritually, the child might be painted on special occasions. One of the most touching of all human ceremonies would have to be the custom among the Arapaho when the child has lost a parent. The little boy or girl is painted in a special ceremony with the family seated around, and the painter speaks to the child in words such as these: "Your life has been made sad, your loss is great. Your father is taken from you. But he will be well, and the Father-Above looks after you. Your life must go on. We will help you." Another version of this exhortation is sung among the Pawnee:

> My dear child, stop crying,
> Yonder there, in the expanse of the heavens, is where
> power dwells.[9]

The passage into youth was also a difficult one, and the Indian child received an appropriately strenuous introduction. Tribes across North America sent children at the age of seven or eight (before puberty, when visions were no longer pure) into the wilderness to fast and to endure solitude. The first stay might have been only twelve hours,

[9] Densmore, *Pawnee Music*, S. I., Bulletin 93 (1929), p. 113.

but later could last as long as ten days and nights with no food and little water while the child waited for the vision of the direction of his or her life. When the vision finally came (in former times—this is not often practiced at present), the child was brought home with rejoicing and a feast was held. Now the child had a special patron among the Powers—an eagle, a wolf, a bear, or whatever had come to it in the hallucinatory state. Again, girls experiencing their first periods were sacred and even a source of terror to men. It was a time of "shame," but also of special communion with the supernatural.

A Catholic priest once recalled an experience among the Oglala Sioux, where he still works, in which an old man gave a talk to Indian high school students. He mused, "Perhaps it is good that we no longer do many of these hard things—fasting, solitude, hanging from the pole— perhaps. But what do we have in its place to temper and test the character of our people? This is why we have alcoholism and quarreling and decay. We give our people no challenges, nothing except despair. This is why we are dying." The Indians are reviving many of these customs in some places. The need of a challenge calls them, not perhaps any longer to build the fierce Sioux warrior so admired by Erik Erikson, but to face whatever twentieth-century life holds.

The period of middle life in traditional tribal religion consists of all the things relating to replenishing the people. The family man or woman becomes a member of some lodge or society, meeting certain requirements to do so. Courtship and marriage are carefully guarded by religious sanctions which I shall describe later on. A man becomes adept at tribal rituals, and may repeatedly endure the Sun Dance. The values inculcated in childhood are developed:

respect for property but simultaneous readiness to use property for the common good and not, save in some rare tribal traditions, for self-advancement. The hunter learns to deal respectfully with his quarry, regretful that he must kill in order to live himself.[10] It is worth remarking here that today there is a great absence of orderly progress in identity among Indians, especially men. The years which should be so productive are often wasted. It is among men beyond forty or even fifty that we see most constructive activity, worldly or religious. Younger men in their twenties and early thirties are struggling for this lost identity that they had when, in older days, it was the young man's duty to go on the hunt and to protect the tribe—a duty in fact that often prohibited marriage until this term of service ended. There is new optimism, however, in various programs that are making use of the talents of younger men, and the restoration of old rites are having their impact.

The butte of old age is hard to climb and hard to walk across. Besides the physical hardships, there is the realization that there are no more buttes to climb—in this world. The treatment of the aged seems to have varied greatly from tribe to tribe. In some tribes they were respected but not well cared for by the younger men. Sometimes among the migratory tribes, the sheer hardships of journeying demanded that the old be left behind to die. Some peoples, too, resented old people because they reminded them of the sacrifices they would have to make at the coming death-rites and afterward. And still, in nearly all the tribes there was a sense of respect which was a product of religious faith. First of all, the aged were recognized as repositories of sacred knowledge and wisdom, from whom valuable

---

[10] On this, for informative details, see Hartley Burr Alexander, *The World's Rim* (Lincoln: University of Nebraska Press, 1969), p. 184.

learning could be obtained. Second, the aged were so close to the next world that they had a unique quality of holiness, which in my own experience younger Arapaho still recognize. It is obvious here, too, how a breakdown in religious tradition can lead to a whole society's coming to see its aged as useless. They can no longer do hard work, and technology has often passed them by; so, with no particular wisdom to communicate and no special nearness to a life with God that their juniors might revere, the old person is simply discarded. Finally, at the far edge of the fourth butte is the passage into the unknown. The Indian has traditionally faced it with faith in some form of a life to come. I close this chapter by citing another Pawnee prayer, given for one who has passed over the edge. It is said by the mythical hero-twins as they cremate the body of their father: "Father, we used to love you but now we are going to burn you up and the smoke will ascend to Tirawa; but, Father, you are not dead forever, and someday we will see you again." [11]

[11] Densmore, *Pawnee Music*, p. 107.

Chapter Three

Life at the Center

THE ETHICAL AND SOCIAL DIMENSIONS

My kindred, there remains one more matter, something I want to say for you to bear well in mind. It is said traditionally, when anyone on Good meditates in his heart, there is formed the thought. And when he thinks of Good it is easy to behave well, but when he misbehaves it is the Evil that a person seriously thinks about as concerns his life. It is exceedingly hard because it is necessary that we prepare the soul-spirit in order that we shall be able to take it back home again to where it belongs, to our father, when its use is finished here where we live. Here in this place it is the body that shall remain here because here is where it belongs on the ground. . . .

> Address of the Master of Ceremonies,
> Delaware Big House Ceremony[1]

And this is the judgment, that the light has come into the world, and men have loved darkness rather than light, because their deeds were evil. For every one who does evil hates the light, and does not come to the light, lest his deeds should be exposed. But he who does what is true comes to the light, that it may be clearly seen that his deeds have been wrought in God.

> John 3:19–21, RSV

[1] Quoted by Margot Astrov, ed., *American Indian Prose and Poetry, an Anthology* (New York: John Day, 1972), p. 169.

81

It has been said by some writers that most Indians cannot accept the Christian doctrines of sin and guilt because such teachings are so foreign to their mentality. On the contrary, though, it is more likely that what the Indians rejected was a narrow puritanical or highly Europeanized mode of presentation. Those who deny that Indians could accept a doctrine of sin—"original" or "personal"—are speaking, I suggest, from a restricted notion of the word "sin." That Indians could never accept man as "naturally sinful," as Ruth Underhill writes, is not only probably true but describes the attitude of great numbers of Christians as well. Man is not "naturally sinful," but "sins" because of a mysterious and demonic foreign element in his being. His sin is indeed an act of freedom, but it is not intended by the Creator.[2] In other words, that man needs redemption seems to me a constant element of Indian belief. I would even venture to say that there has never been a group of people more ready to face the reality of moral evil as well as good, and so prayerfully desirous of doing that good.

That human virtue and vice exercise their effect in man's cosmos, and that ethical conduct is thus closely related to a cosmological sense, is not only Indian, but the teaching of many Christian theologians as well. Thus, Karl Rahner writes of the human soul as intimately related, through the body, to the entire cosmos, so that any good action or any evil action reverberates throughout that world—as Indians might say, against God, self, fellow man, and the very uni-

[2] Underhill, *Red Man's Religion* (Chicago: University of Chicago Press, 1965), p. 254. We have already seen how some tribes mythologize the presence of death in the world. Paul Radin records a Pawnee myth in which death's origin is definitely moral: men are condemned to die— a fate not otherwise decreed for them—when they offend Heaven by slaying the sacred wolf, the first animal to share the earth with them. Surely here we behold sin "at the origin." Cf. Radin, *op. cit.,* pp. 265-268.

verse itself. Man's life after death, when no physical body stands between the soul and the world to insulate it, is determined by the kind of relationship it developed while in the body. Such thinking is typical of the apparently universal Indian image of man living in a centered world where he can increase or destroy its harmony.

Another preliminary remark to our discussion is the observation that for the traditional Indian, personal individual morality *is* social morality. There is no boxing-off of two separate categories. Even the celebrated individualism of the plains warriors or hunters was entirely taken for granted as conducive to the tribal well-being. If an individual performed well, the whole community would benefit, and if he was selfish, not only would the tribe suffer but he, too, as virtually an organic part of the body would suffer. As should be evident, the Pauline notion of the Body of Christ is very close to such a doctrine of solidarity.

RELIGION AND TRIBAL JUSTICE

In general, religious sanctions, such as existed apart from punitive external sanctions, were aimed at developing the personal-social instincts. If there *was* a belief in the idea of life after death, this notion was applied to punishment centered around crimes against the commonweal. For this reason, tribal penal practice was often tied in with religious festivals.

A fascinating aspect of the Green Corn festival of the Florida Seminole was the built-in method of guaranteeing the community well-being.[3] If a member was caught in one

[3] Capron, "The Medicine Bundles of the Florida Seminole and the Green Corn Dance," S. I., Bulletin 151 (1953), pp. 196–198.

of the more grievous antisocial actions, his trial and judgment, acquittal or punishment took a religious form that
would certainly impress modern penal reformers. The attitude was both environmental, in that it considered the
guilty party's social situation, and personal, in that finally it
did not absolve him of personal accountability. The as-
sumption regarding a proven criminal was not that the
person was "sinful" but that he was sick, deranged, or perhaps possessed. This must be the case, was the reasoning,
because these very harmful deeds against his people could
finally only mean tribal disintegration and his own personal destruction. Thus, the trial and/or punishment was
also a ritual in which the medicine man strove to exorcise
the guilty party of his wrong attitude and get him to admit,
under considerable pressure, that he was possessed. If he
did finally yield to this technique—and apparently most
malefactors did—he was reinstated in the tribe.

Thus the primary purpose of these rituals was to rehabili-
tate a victim of personal disorder. If the person relapsed,
he might endure the same ordeal again, and even three or
four times. Finally, however, if he proved incorrigible the
tribal judges would come to a decision that he was a men-
ace to the common welfare. In a silent rite, the oldest man
on the council was designated executioner and given a
weapon, in the case described a shotgun, and sent to carry
out the sentence. It is noted that the condemned man did
not try to resist when he saw the old man coming, and took
the shot full in the chest.

Every tribe had its own way of ritualizing its obligations.
Hilger describes how in former nomadic days the Arapaho
camped according to *gentes,* or tribal clans.[4] Other tribes

---

[4] Hilger, *Arapaho Child Life*, p. 192.

were divided into what we call bands. These divisions were symbolized in some way by the mode of living, for example among the Arapaho by the ever-present and meaningful camp-circle. Everyone who lived within this circle seems to have seen it as a sacred hoop, and knew that if one violated one's proper role, the hoop might be destroyed. Thus, there were ways of protecting property, guarding against sexual abuses among the young, and very elaborately detailed rules against intermarriage within the clan. While promiscuity was generally frowned on, it was not punished by law; adultery, however, was a very serious matter because of the havoc it could wreak among a people so dependent on one another. An unfaithful wife might be forced to live with her lover, or more severely, might have her face disfigured by her husband and be sent off to the intruder. Apart from having to receive the wife, however, the guilty male does not seem to have faced external sanctions other than being condemned by the people and avoided.

With the upheaval of religion and culture and the confinement of tribes to reservations, religiously sanctioned tribal justice has suffered probably irreparable damage, at least among most tribes outside certain compact and well-insulated groups like the Pueblo. Reservation police now have to follow the American penal system, and tribal councils or courts are tightly restricted in most cases by Indian agencies. There is, of course, no more tribal circle outside the times of pow-wows and religious ceremonies. Among plains tribes, even new housing projects built possibly to duplicate the old tribal symbolism have become miniature ghettos because the laws governing them are the still-alien laws of white society, and not the more internalized sanctions of a unified people. Some internalizing of law and morality in a religious context does still take place in the various religious festivals, but these at present are disjointed and often unrelated to the life of the tribe as a whole. It is, of course, wrong to utterly condemn or exonerate our predecessors, since we ourselves would not likely have been more insightful, but much of the present situation can be attributed to past governmental and missionary attitudes.

INDIVIDUAL AND SOCIAL DEVELOPMENT

Degrees of individualism and its relation to social consciousness vary according to tribes or locales, with the individual more glorified among the plains Indians and the group among the agricultural tribes. However, religious asceticism across the board can be seen to have a profound effect on the individual's growth and indirectly on that of the tribe. We have already seen how great an emphasis was placed on solitary vision-seeking. But today too, among many tribes, great value is given to the fasting of individuals in a communal ritual context. As one watches the Sun Dance Pledger and his fellow dancers undergoing their ordeal, he is struck by the fact that each one must suffer as an individual before God. Many dancers will deliberately extend themselves to the extreme edge of endurance, perhaps reminiscent of former days of personal warrior prowess, perhaps an effort to gain greater favor from the Creator through suffering. While the torture of suspension is practiced only sparingly now, mostly among the Sioux, one does still see Indian people who bear the scars of personal offerings of flesh from arms or chest, marks considered sacred because they represent offerings to the Creator. Ritual scratching of the arms was still undergone by the Seminole in the 1940s as a witness to endurance and generosity.

Yet, amid this highly individual asceticism, we also see examples of lofty social awareness. Rites like the calumet rituals are social, and the newer Ghost Dance and Native Amercain Church show evidence of a socio-religious mentality made sharper by suffering. The most impressive of these signs are the records of public confessions in the peyote rituals. In the case of the Sun Dance, too, the individual's vow is very often, if not usually, taken for the welfare of another person—a sick relative, a son at war, a friend or relation in trouble. Occasionally it happens that a man dies or is killed before he is able to carry out a vow; then a relative or friend will often take the burden upon himself.

Throughout the Sun Dance trial, the sufferer has strong social support—a grandfather who looks after his every need (except, of course, food or drink), who cools him, bathes him, and paints him. Tribal members stand around for hours in sun and wind to pray with him and share some of his endurance. Shouts of encouragement can be heard as the dance goes on, and jokes are exchanged among the dancers. Many women standing or seated around in the "forecourt" of the lodge sing or actually weep for the participants. One of the moral exhortations that accompanies Indian ritual is that its effect should be longer lasting, in more frequent self-discipline and daily prayer. In former times when tribal life was more bound together by religion, this kind of control was a simpler matter.

The personal qualities inculcated in Indian behavior and

character by traditional religious life, or by social customs having a religious sanction, were hospitality, a basic respect for the aged, kindness to the weak and to animals, stamina, generosity, reserve, and affection between husband and wife. Polygamy, which might seem contrary to such a moral code, was allowed and even commonplace, but the understanding was, as it was among the Moslems, that a man must be able to care for his wives properly. Some tribes did have provisions for a man to marry his wife's sisters, but this seems to be looked back upon with disfavor by later generations. The strong communitarian instinct can be seen in the custom (not requirement) in many tribes of a levirate or sororate marriage: a man might marry his dead brother's wife or a woman her dead sister's husband in order to raise up children to the departed, as was the custom with the ancient Hebrews.

On reading the various accounts and monographs by explorers and anthropologists, what strikes one is the almost universal hospitality shown by Indian tribes, especially to their white visitors. It is quite remarkable as described in David Bushnell's writings about explorers and missionaries among the Siouan, Algonquian, and Caddoan tribes west of the Mississippi.[5] Unless Bushnell is suppressing information, which is hardly likely, there are practically no examples of inhospitable or harsh treatment rendered to Whites. On the contrary, the tribal leaders went out of their way to receive these visitors as special guests. There seems to have been a conviction among the Indians,

[5] David I. Bushnell, Jr., *Burials of the Algonquian, Siouan and Caddoan Tribes West of the Mississippi*, S. I., Bulletin 83 (1927), and *Villages of the Algonquian, Siouan and Caddoan Tribes West of the Mississippi*, S. I., Bulletin 77.

at least until the middle of the nineteenth century, that they and the newcomers could share the land equally, even if the land was sometimes thought to be the tribe's sacred inheritance. This spirit of welcome was, of course, wearing a bit thin by the time of the gold rushes and railroad drives.

Generosity, especially among the western Algonquian tribes, is practiced, according to white standards, almost to excess. I have already written about lavish gift-giving as an integral part of Sun Dance worship. Alfred Kroeber, whose anthropological career spanned the first half of the present century, noted this generosity in 1903. It is not unusual for an Arapaho to give a friend a valuable piece of clothing, a rifle, jewelry, even a horse simply as a sign of friendship. In some sense it is assumed that the beneficiary would and will on some occasion offer a similar gift. With the many ritual occasions for this, situations for reciprocity arise rather often. The same spirit, I suspect, that animates a person to offer even pieces of his own flesh to the Great Spirit also moves him readily to renounce proprietorship over possessions. The problems generated by such a culture's clash with capitalism are evident at once—unless one happened to be a member of that famous "capitalistic" society, the Kwakiutl of the western coastlands. This tribe did apparently put great store by possessions, and its ritual *potlatch* was by no means generosity but a way of outmaneuvering an opponent into relinquishing property to the giver in a contest of accumulated "givable" wealth. But here, too, one had to play by the rules, and the rules were ritualized. It has been remarked how great the potential might have been for mutual-benefit societies if the practice had been developed and encouraged by white missions.

Respect and kindness to the aged seem to have been

trained into Arapaho children from infancy. Such respect was apparently widespread among Indian tribes, granted the occasions of neglect or abandonment spoken of earlier. Often, such abandonment was simply a matter of survival for those still young and vigorous, such as in severe food shortages or on those frozen treks across the northern woods and prairies. But in general the attitude was one of consideration for others weaker than oneself. In Arapaho tribal life over recent years, respect and concern for grandparents has been most evident, and seldom is an elderly person placed in a home unwillingly. Unfortunately, some tribes are so fragmented that reservation care cannot be given to the aged, so that the crisis of the elderly touches these tribes as it has white society. But it was not just an arbitrary bit of terminology that traditionally the highest deities below the Creator were four old men, and the sun and moon were often grandfather and grandmother.

The gentle treatment accorded to animals by Indians is legendary, and seldom is even the lowest form of animal life badly treated. If the white visitor to Indian homes is an animal lover, he will feel especially at ease. Generally the home and surroundings have an abundance of dogs, cats, horses, and other pets brought in from the wilds. In ancient times it seems to have been the practice for the mother of a newborn child, until her colostrum was safe for the baby to drink, to be nursed by a newborn raccoon or fox, which then became the pet of the growing child.

We can realize how the Indian's closeness to nature made his at-home-ness with animals second nature to him and such a great part of his native religion. There are prayers typical of this attitude in which a man grieves over a dead whale, or a woman supplicates a cedar tree she must cut.

The mythical sources for this reverence help us further to understand the Indian's habit of direct address to nature and even his mystical experiences, which we shall study in the next chapter.

Indian sexual mores in general had elaborate safeguards, some of which, regarding puberty and menstruation, we have already discussed. The contemporary trend toward "desacralizing" sex would never have been understood in traditional Indian societies. As with everything mysterious, matters dealing with the origin of human life were surrounded by ritual, which had nothing to do with puritanism. The traditional Indian attitude would confirm the judgment of most contemporary anthropologists and sociologists that where sex is taken casually and with no seriousness, and accompanied by no safeguards and disciplines, guilt, fear, and insecurity are the results. It is at least a valid working hypothesis that such insecurities stem not from puritanical or guilt-ridden religious training, but from a failure to appreciate the depth of the mystery of human origins.

It is recorded of most Indian groups that they had customs to control premarital courtship, and that these customs had a definite ritualistic nature. Among the Chippewa tribes, men were considered marriageable only when they could provide for a family, and women when they showed the ability to maintain a household. During courtship girls were kept constantly in the presence of their mothers. However, among some Sioux tribes, girls were even tied down at night as they slept in their tipis—which would indicate that we are not talking here about any stylized WASP Victorian culture! Boys and girls never went out alone together, and if a boy wanted to court a girl he went by daylight to see her in the presence of her parents. If a young man's intentions were serious, he went through a prescribed rite, beginning by talking with the older people of the family, who lived near the door of the lodge. This done, he could then progress to the middle of the lodge, where the girl lived, and they might talk quietly together—but always observed. At other times it was customary for the suitor to sit near the lodge, playing the "courting flute" as his intended listened from inside the lodge. The courtly and chivalric overtone of this idyll is augmented by the fact that often the youth would seek love charms from the tribal medicine man. The desire to marry was shown by the youth's killing a deer or some other game and bringing it to the girl's parents, thus indicating his ability and intention to be a good provider. Parents would then strive to learn all they could about the young man, and if they liked him, he might begin a guarded and chaperoned marriage-courtship.[6]

We find similar customs among the plains tribes, in many cases with a delicate subtlety and humor pervading them. Among the Arapaho a girl would set the flap of the family tipi to indicate her interest in a young man. One recalls with delight Black Elk's story of the lovesick young brave and the stern protective future father-in-law who forced the youth to do difficult tasks to win his bride. Likewise, among many tribes, elaborate precautions were taken so that brothers and sisters (and first cousins, too) never or rarely spoke to one another after puberty, except indirectly and by an intermediary. The custom has largely vanished, but the reserve can still be seen.

[6] For much of this information, I am indebted to Inez Hilger's monograph on Chippewa and Arapaho child life, esp. pp. 156ff. in *Chippewa Child Life*.

All such customs were of course at times honored in the breach, for elopements were possible, and sometimes children would be born out of wedlock. It is an equally remarkable sign of the flexibility of Indian cultures that when this happened it was regretted and frowned upon, but the child was not discriminated against, other than that it was called something like "sweetheart child" at birth. Today, on reservations where Indian ways are following white ways and the number of "sweetheart children" is increasing, it is still edifying to see how readily the families accept the child and care for it. This is not to rationalize an unfortunate situation, but similarly one cannot help but be impressed that pregnant unwed mothers seldom if ever procure abortions. Such is also in the tradition, which, long before Christianity, frowned upon induced abortions and generally gave an aborted fetus the honor of full burial rites.

Marriage was usually carried out by a simple ceremony, if it could be called a ceremony at all. The couple simply ate together, and shared a fur robe for bedding, while the man went to live with the woman's family—again seemingly a widely prevalent custom—for about a year, after which the couple lived independently. There are records of young women being given to men they did not know, or to old men, but an equal number of witnesses indicate that a girl's feelings were generally respected and that she was free to refuse a suitor. There was no law that held marriage indissoluble, and often husbands and wives would separate, free to remarry after a certain period of time. Sadly but predictably enough, most of these customs, as with the case of adultery, were more burdensome for the woman than for the man.

MYTHS AS MORALITY TALES

We have already discussed Indian myths and legends under the rubric of religious instruction, moral exhortation,
and entertainment. We do not always find it easy to ascer-
tain the difference, especially between the entertaining and
the ethical. However, even in what we would call the most
vulgar or obscene stories,[7] the offending parties usually got
their just deserts. Such tales were generally told in a ritual
context before they passed on into popular conversation.
Some of the examples indicate a profound moral sense, especially toward what one might think of as a certain primitive "natural law" founded on the instinct that nature
responds in kind.

There are many Indian tribes whose lore includes the
legends of the water-monsters, the great unknown of the
depths. Even today Indian children on the Wind River
Reservation delight in spook stories about the "Big Foot"
who likes to eat people; but this kind of tale is related to
much more serious myths. Marriot and Rachlin recount a
Cheyenne story that reaches into the very roots of Indian
spirituality.[8] In abbreviated form, the tale is that fifty
young warriors and braves in the days before the coming
of the horse set out hunting. After a long, exhausting, and

[7] Anthropologists around the turn of this century were generally required to render these stories, given them by interpreters or translated
by themselves, into the Latin language to satisfy museum officials or
obscenity codes. This bit of legislation has bequeathed to American
literary history, for those who can read Latin, a howlingly funny minor
literary genre.

[8] Alice Marriot and Carol K. Rachlin, *American Indian Mythology*
(New York: Thomas Y. Crowell, 1968), pp. 41–45.

fruitless expedition, they were making their way through the yucca flats of the Staked Plains, where poles had been driven into the ground to aid travelers in finding water in the raw country of western Oklahoma. Upon spying a shining object in the distance they at first thought it was nothing but a mirage. But the young men soon realized that this was no ordinary mirage; it was more like a giant, shining mound. As is the case with any such sacred phenomenon, some of the men were greatly alarmed at it while others wanted to approach it. Discovering that the object was moving along the path to a waterhole, the men decided to follow it. Upon drawing closer, they saw that it was a giant shining water turtle. The beast moved seemingly unconcerned along the staked trail, beckoning to no one, but trudging purposefully "as if it were a person." "I'm going to go for a ride on its back," said one young man, and he climbed aboard the animal as it lumbered along. The others, seized by the spirit of adventure also clambered atop the shining shell—all but one, the chief, who walked cautiously alongside.

Not content merely to ride the monster, the youths began to try to torment and injure it, curious about its great strength and imperturbability. But the more they teased it, striking it with their bone knives and stone axes, the more relentlessly did it inch forward, slowly, slowly making its way. The chief kept begging the men to get off the monster, but they were too busy arguing among themselves to pay attention to the chief. Was the turtle divinely sent, to be reverenced as a benevolent deity or messenger? Or was it possessed of dangerous demonic power and best left alone?

But when those who had come to fear the turtle tried to dismount, they found themselves stuck fast to its back.

Their panic spread to the others, and all found themselves unable to get free of the beast. The men cried out to their chief to help them, and the chief in turn made supplications to the turtle as he ran alongside: "Let our men go and they will forever hold you in honor!" But the turtle, unharmed by axes and knives, gave no sign of response, merely lumbering inexorably along, much to the horror of the men, who realized that it would soon enter the huge watering hole opening up before them. Then the chief, accepting their fate, said, "I have done all that I can do. Something wonderful was shown to you, and you did not respect it. Now you will be punished because you thought wrong in your hearts. I cannot change anything." As the turtle began its descent into the lake, the youths became resigned to their imminent deaths and called upon the chief to return to the tribe and establish a mourning period for them. This the tribe did, but when they returned to the scene the next year all they found was a deep, dry hole full of bones. Contrary to what geologists say—that these remains are just the bones of long-dead animals—the old Indians know differently.

Rudolf Otto, in *The Idea of the Holy,* made it a point to stress that the holy—whatever man finds mysterious, awesome, fascinating, and frightening—is so much beyond man's powers of conception that it transcends even his moral codes. He went on to stress, however, that the holy is also a value in itself, a position we see supported above in a classic parable of mystery as value. The unknown is terrifying, and if men would dare to probe it, they must take their chances. If they are arrogant in their quest, the mystery will claim them for its own and perhaps destroy them. Nature to Indians has always been sacred; it is to be dealt with subtly and gently, lest it retaliate not with hateful vengeance but with the silently ponderous impassivity of the giant turtle. To picture the Indian as a lovesick suitor of nature is, of course, a sentimental fallacy. The relationship was not that of the idyll of an all-benign cosmos, but the often terrible experience of hunger, thirst, storms and floods, wild beasts defending their own prerogatives, and freakish upheavals in the earth.

Still today, this sense of sacredness is powerful; many Indians are suspicious of man's probing of outer space and his trampling across the face of the moon especially when there is so much to be improved right here on earth. Even younger Indians will not tamper with relics or burial articles they might find in the hills. A few years ago one generally heard such a mentality written off as the superstition or "magicalism" of a primitive world-view. Today, the implicit word of warning from ecologists is to appreciate the deeper sense of myths relating to the spirits of the forests, the waters, and the skies.

We have observed how easily the characters of Indian mythology change from human to beast and back again, so that frequently the reader or listener cannot determine which form is "real." Examples of this are so numerous that there is no need to dwell on them again; we have already discussed the ancient Indian realization that man is indeed an animal and the offspring of animals, however special an animal he is. The legends are full of love affairs between man and dog, woman and bear, man and buffalo cow.

One Arapaho myth is worth singling out as an example. In the version recorded by Dorsey and Kroeber, a hunter happens upon a female buffalo caught in a mud wallow. He helps her out of trouble, and then has intercourse with her, after which he takes her home as his wife. Soon a child is born to the couple. But the man, or in some versions his relatives, treat the buffalo woman and her child harshly, and the pair flee back to the herd. Some recountings show the woman departing and the man following, according to the custom of marrying into the woman's family line. When the man in his pursuit comes upon the buffalo herd and goes to the buffalo chief to reclaim his woman, he is given a number of challenges to overcome: endurance, minor torments, and finally single combat with the chief or one of his great warriors. The man slays his adversary, who then comes back to life, ready to grant him his bride. Here the chief also bestows on the man the commission to be lord over the buffalo. Whereas, before, the buffalo had been a human flesheater, he would now be a vegetarian, running over the plains with his head down seeking food, while man would now chase after him for his own sustenance.

Some of these stories end with a long ritualistic account of how the subdued chief sends his buffalo-boy grandson as a messenger to the conqueror, begging him to reconstruct him into a new buffalo body. So the man sends back articles and implements of daily use to make the buffalo to his own specifications: bowstrings for sinews, tent poles for bones, stones for hooves, braided rope for a tail, and so on for the entire body down to the last detail. Man had become full lord of the plains.

We can call this type of story an "alienation" myth because it not only narrates origins but rationalizes for guilty man *why* he must slay his brother the buffalo. The details of how carefully primeval man constructs the buffalo point out graphically why the buffalo for the plains Indians was not just a source of food, but an essential ingredient in sustaining his life. It was in fact much more even than this, but the practical value was a convenient measure of its worth. Older Indians today still recall, either through their parents or maybe personal experience, how delicately their people used the animal world and nature. They will recount how the old Indians used every bit of the buffalo as a precious commodity—the hide for clothing and shelter, the meat and marrow and innards for food, the bones for tools and weapons, the sinews for bowstrings. It is easier to understand at times like this the heartbreak and rage that must have seized Indian people on the plains as they observed the unthinking and wholesale slaughter of the buffalo, and the crime of leaving the carcass to rot on the prairie. Where was the Center of the universe in a man who would do such things?

While the economy of nature was perhaps the Indian's dominant moral code, his ethics also included instruction in the evil of certain antisocial actions. Thus, the old storytellers dramatized graphically for their young listeners the many morality tales governing those social bonds that no tribe could do without. Fables condemning incest are common, and the act is so heinous that it is generally described as being committed by someone of another tribe. In one long series of myths, a woman given to adultery, deception, and murder is finally slain for her crimes by her husband. Another sequence of stories tells of an interloper, possibly a trickster type of fiend, who dupes an innocent young pregnant wife (who after the fashion of Grimm's tales is disobedient to her husband and invites the intruder in) and cuts her open, tossing the fetus onto the ground. But these two crimes do not go unpunished. The aborted child, or twin sons in some versions, is not dead, and rises to search out the villain and destroy him. There follows a ceremony in which father and sons place the dead mother in a Sweat Lodge and shoot four arrows into the ground around it, thus restoring her to life. Other stories revolved around a cruel and selfish young husband who refused to provide for his aged in-laws; the old parents miraculously discovered a blood clot which became a boy who grew up to care for them in their need.

Obviously, all Indians were not paragons of the ethical life, but they did believe in a strong connection between the sense of wholeness given by religious identity and the sound moral teaching that results. Religion does not automatically lead to virtuous living; it can even lead to perversion. Nor could one maintain that the nonreligious person will necessarily be morally deficient; nevertheless the sense of unity with God, self, man, and the cosmos that a genuine religious response affords will open a person or society to basic human values. William James maintained this a half century ago when he singled out as one of the concomitants of religious experience the engendering of loving affection and a healthy relation to the world.

But the catastrophic historical fact remains for the Indian people. As Black Elk sadly commented, the nation's hoop is broken now and there is no more Center. The shock has been massive, perhaps comparable only to an invasion of the present world by beings from another planet who would destroy all the former means of cultural support; forms of worship would, in such an analogy, be interdicted and social existence reduced to an impoverished imitation of the mores of the conquerors. The Center has indeed been broken. And yet, as Black Elk also said, the Center is where you find it, and it is not too late for an oppressed culture to use its many available resources and the helps to be found in the dominant culture to re-construct the sacred hoop. Such elements include the religion, the tribal wisdom traditions (which bear so much resemblance to the Book of Proverbs), respect for nature and persons, and the self-knowledge that has traditionally come to them through asceticism.

Chapter Four

Holiness and Power

THE EXPERIENTIAL DIMENSION

The yellow star has noticed me,
Furthermore it gave me a standing yellow feather,
That yellow star.

Pawnee Ghost Dance Song[1]

Then I saw a new heaven and a new earth. . . .

Revelation 21:1, RSV

The Pawnee song quoted above was composed by the singer upon awakening from a trance during the Ghost Dance. It was a dream of a yellow star coming to give him a yellow feather, and saying, "All the stars in the sky are people." It was a highly favored vision, frustrated by events of 1890, but still a source of light and hope for the future amid the decay and disaster of that period. The selection from Revelation is part of the apocalyptic vision of the seer, who saw the new dispensation arising out of the destruction of the old order of things, and it is remarkably like some of the visions of Black Elk.

Indian religious conversation seems to draw a very close equivalence, though not through identical words, between the notions of "holy" and "powerful" and the relationship

---

[1] Frances Densmore, *Pawnee Music*, S. I., Bulletin 93 (1929), p. 83.

of both to spirit. To experience spirit is to experience power, as when, for example, their fellow tribespeople regard the Sun Dance devotees as both holy and filled with special power. Such a notion of holiness, as we have noted, is the usual experience of the deeply religious person. To be holy is not first of all to be virtuous but to be "sacred" or set apart, full of awesome power, able to inspire wonder, even fear. Some modern Christian theologians have attempted to explain that a thing can be holy without being sacred, because God created and hallowed all things. Indian religion would never deny such an assertion, but it does always affirm a special quality in holy things. However much everyday life is hallowed, therefore, the experience of the sacred is not everyday life; it is the trance of the Ghost Dance, the faster's vision, the wonder of the sunrise, or the vision of a new world order. And it is worth adding that for Indian thought, a dream or trance is not an *unconscious* state but a state of heightened awareness.

The question of a more sophisticated age, when it hears about a vision or a sacred experience, is, "Was it *real,* or was it drug-induced or auto-suggestion, or just the creative imagination?" The question is legitimate. The masters of Christian spirituality from the desert fathers through Teresa of Ávila and Ignatius Loyola always sought to discern what kind of spirit was moving the person, or whether it was a spirit at all. The question extends itself further to the difficult task of determining when a gifted person has received contemplation "infused" by God or when the vision is simply a product of the imagination, or a combination of each.

The old Indian sages certainly did not accept everyone who claimed to be a visionary, but for them it was not a question of whether the experience came from the imagination or subconscious archetypes or from God or the spirits, because there was no ultimate distinction in affective experience between the sacral and the world powers; the "holy" was simply a greater intensification, given in a special situation, of the order in which all of us live. While it was indeed an experience "set apart," it does not seem to have been the "wholly other" described by Otto. It was an endowment of the Spirit as power. God alone was *beyond* this power, as witness the general conception that He was in heaven, usually outside of all experience. It took special messengers to bring the word of God to man.

This Indian notion is similar to that of some modern theologians: if faith tells a person that he lives not in a profane order but in a created supernatural one, then he does not torture his mind overmuch about the nature of a particular vision or prophetic inspiration. Such a "logic of faith" tells him that if the experience indicates both individual and communal welfare, there is no need for concern as to whether or not it is directly supplied by God. This, of course, does not remove the uncertainty involved in the speculative analysis of religious experience, nor does it resolve the problems relating to such "bizarre" modes of obtaining the experience as drugs and severe asceticism. But it does help one understand the religious mentality of a world where one is in constant touch with the Powers.

In the whole area of religious experience, one must, of course, write more than ever as an "outsider" seeking understanding of the American Indian culture. This is true of any religious tradition, but it is preeminently the case with Indian religion, which is reluctant to speak about the tradition in general and more particularly about one's personal experiences. The very practice of secrecy is a product of the belief that in religious visions one's communion with the Powers can be lost through irreverent divulgence. This caution is contagious. After attendance at Indian ceremonies or listening to Indian prayers, one will often find himself handling religious objects and participating in rituals with greater care. It is not legalism or a dry rubricalism, but a feeling that there *is* a certain "medicine" in the very things and gestures of Indian ritual, and this does affect communion with God.

THE IMPORTANCE OF THE SENSES

Many Indians have stressed in conversation how important it is to touch the instruments of religious worship. This does not suggest that they will not at times refrain from touching certain sacred objects and persons, but the overall action of worship has to engage the tactile senses: sight, hearing, and smell. This does not always or even generally parallel the rather superficial message conveyed by contemporary cults of "touch me," but rather, entails a contact that often causes pain and demands tremendous endurance and hardship. If the Indian mentality is to some extent what may be conventionally labeled "romantic," as I have suggested, that romanticism does not pick and choose where it will respond, but submits itself totally to the overtures of nature, whether tranquillizing or terrifying.

In recent years, the Indian religious experience most popularized, especially since the appearance of the works of Carlos Castaneda, is the drug experience, which in North America is restricted mostly to the ritual use of peyote. Even my limited acquaintance with the peyote cult convinces me of how poorly it is understood by those who consider it either wild licentious practice or mere indulgence in a "high." A peyote meeting is an elaborately prepared service, by now fairly uniformly stylized across North America.[2] The tipi is constructed at sunrise the previous day, so that the entrance will directly face the new sun as the rite comes to completion. Participants enter the tipi at sundown and prepare for a night of sitting on the bare ground. They must endure the fire and smoke from which the gradual buildup of ashes is made, to create the image of the legendary Waterbird, patron symbol of the Native American Church. The worshipers receive periodic helpings of the plant—generally four buttons or a pinch at a time. It is a bitter substance and often causes nausea, at least to those whose hearts are not truly involved in the worship. Water can be drunk only after midnight, because early contact with the plant and water together can cause severe illness. The participants also rub themselves with the traditional sage, smoke cigarettes rolled from cornshucks (if available) or paper and Bull Durham tobacco.

For the peyote people the attendant rites make the coming of heightened consciousness, the spontaneous prayers and listening to the songs and drums, the sense of unity and the resolve to reform one's life a genuine reward for endurance and hardship. Thus, as with other consciousness-heightening drugs, the accompanying circumstances and actions are as important as—possibly even more important than—the drug itself. Castaneda correctly warned off from

[2] Weston LaBarre, in his book *The Peyote Cult* (Hamden, Conn.: The Shoestring Press, 1964), gives a detailed history and scientific study of the movement.

Indian magic usages those who were merely curious or just "heads." One must have a genuinely religious motive for entering the meeting tent, along with a pure and prayerful heart.

Careful attention to detail is in itself conducive to religious experience. Painting of bodies is done with great care and exactness; incense is used with elaborate concern, as patterns are followed which the participants hope are imitations of the way it was done by "the old ones." Again, it is not a matter of legalism, but of religious "medicine." The experience of carefully enacted ritual, as the Zen masters make clear, can be an exercise in tranquil self-discipline and "right absorption." The practice of prayer, the bowed head, ceremonial weeping become "efficacious signs" that bring about what they signify.

When Indians take part in a Sweat Lodge ceremony, the religious experience takes several forms. One hears occasional jokes at other times that the Sweat Lodge is just a "hot bath," but the actual descriptions suggest much more, because the rite is again one of endurance and prayer. The bathers sit inside with pails of cold water, and steaming hot stones are handed into the lodge. When the water is poured over them, the result is almost intolerably hot. The bather is instructed to pray silently and endure, while the steam gives cleansing and new vigor. It is a rite of the "world Powers," because the power of healing comes from the stones, the heat, and the water. The Seminole retain a special stone that is said to be given this power by God. Alexander devoted a whole essay to the symbolism of "The Abiding Rock" that provides stability to creation and to whose interior energy the healing vapors are due. And Ruth Underhill cites a Sioux Sweat Lodge prayer:

Oh Rocks . . . by receiving your sacred breath
Our People will be long-winded as they walk
The Path of life; your breath [the steam]
Is the very breath of life.[4]

If we combine in our own imaginations the feeling of cleansing sweat, the closeness of a dark cell, the hardness of rock and the breath of silent or whispered prayer, we can gain some understanding of why this very corporeal action can be a personal and communal spiritual experience of considerable intensity.

Among North American Indians, except for the late-nineteenth-century arrival of peyote, a state of higher consciousness was not achieved through drugs. It came, as with Zen training and yoga, through severe self-discipline and self-emptying. The latest Roman Catholic alterations in fast and abstinence requirements were no doubt needed reforms of a type of legalism or empty ritualism for many. But the downplaying of personal asceticism in the name of social and charitable actions, however laudable, can possibly cause Roman Catholics to lose their awareness of the importance to individuals of silence, solitude, fasting, and bodily and mental discipline. All of these values were sought in North American Indian religious experience.

Over the centuries of their lives in the northern climes, silence and solitude have seeped into the very spiritual marrow of the forest and plains peoples. This has nothing to do with a negative attitude toward speech, which is enjoyed and treated with reverence, but rather, with a respect for the mystic void that waits to be filled up. Even though the Indian known to the white person in history is

4 Underhill, *Red Man's Religion* (Chicago: University of Chicago Press, 1965), p. 40.

silent toward him largely out of caution, and far more outgoing at home with his own people, most Indians do seem to have a natural capacity to be silent and to listen. This is part of a long history that is both practical and religious. On the practical level, it is easy to see how a hunting or gathering or agricultural people would be free of addiction to talkativeness. The nature of the work of hunting, fishing, and gathering calls for quiet concentration and silent use of the senses. If one lives long enough in the wilderness, especially in the giant expanses of the North American West, the sheer overwhelming dimensions of the landscape become a wordless command of silence.

However, a skill in rich narrative does grow out of the life of the wilderness, as we know from the creative tradition of American folklore and country music. And as we have seen, this is true also of Indian peoples, with their long evenings listening to some of the greatest raconteurs and mythologists ever known. In fact, many older Indians, given a relaxed atmosphere and an attentive audience, will continue for hours spinning tales, historical and fabulous. But it comes only when the occasion demands it and not before. Indeed, there is an ancient tradition of character-growth among many tribes that tells when to speak much or little. It is generally expected of many peoples that their deportment be one of reticence and freedom from loud and boastful talk. This kind of conduct no doubt related to the standing need of hunters and warriors to practice a strict self-discipline which could be relaxed only on certain occasions. At feasts, on returning from a victory or a successful hunt, during the times of entertainment, and even at certain points of religious observance (much like the rough baiting of the Iroquois Eagle Dance), loud braggadocio and swaggering claims of achievement were expected and warmly appreciated. Something of this is still seen when two men dancing together at a pow-wow intersperse their dance steps with loud whoops and jibes at one another.

Religious reasons for silence are obvious. Jesus Christ went to the mountain to experience the conversation of His Father, as before Him John the Baptist went into the desert. It was in such periods of silence and aloneness that visions came to Zoroaster, Buddha, and Mohammed. When Indians tell of their wilderness fasts of younger days (never of what their *visions* were) they remark on the solitude that often frightened them and at first made them want to return home. But to flee the wilderness was a disgrace, and they knew that they must remain in silence and fasting until their vision finally came. Silence alone is not magic, but it is power; if the watcher endures long enough, and realizes his own poverty, there comes an answer to fill his emptiness.

The practice of severe fasting was never of itself a source of spiritual visions—God alone or the Powers grant these —but it might be the occasion for them. Severe fasting can, of course, simply induce hallucinations, as can self-inflicted pain. Modern Christians do not as a rule include these practices in their religious lives, and often see them merely as medieval aberrations. But one must interpret Indian spirituality very carefully. To begin with, all Christian worship and prayer, except perhaps for extreme puritanism or rigid legalism, attempted to bring its participants to an affective readiness to meet God. Prior to present-day ecumenical sharing of types of worship, Protestants traditionally used music and spontaneous prayer to set the mood, while the "high-church" traditions sought to make use of processions, vestments, and other kinds of display. Thus, while it was understood that "grace" was never an object supplied on demand, it was assumed that it would work in the soul when there was some preparation for it. So likewise, it would be superficial to characterize dreams and visions brought on through solitude, fasting, and torture as mere hallucinations.

In the Sun Dance, as its veterans report, many things happen to the mind; one "does a lot of thinking." It is most unwise to try to intrude upon the domain of these sacred personal lights, visions, and reflections, but there is no doubt here that as the heart is purified by suffering it is readied for the Presence. To cite Ignatius Loyola, spiritual progress comes in proportion to one's readiness to seek self-abnegation in all matters. Thus, what I have been describing in more or less traditional Christian terms is what ancient Indians—and many modern ones—have meant by commerce with the Powers in their visions and vigils.

Finally, there is the power of music to open the heart. I have already spoken of the Offerings Lodge Sunrise Dance and the drumming and singing of various sacred tipi rites. Again, Indians experience singing as power and as communion with the spirit world: music pleases the Powers as well as human beings, and a special rapport is thus created in its performance. Experience bears out how much traditional music means to Indians when one sees how they can listen or sing for many hours on end, caught up in a near trance, while most Whites, even music lovers, will grow tired of their favorite music after two or three hours.

Those persons able to read music can consult the renditions of Indian song made by Frances Densmore and Alice Fletcher, and many recordings of Indian music are now on the market. All human emotions are expressed in these, especially exhilaration, sadness, and romantic affection. Most religious music differs markedly from the rousing and exuberant drumming and singing of pow-wow music. The impression given by the steady beat of the Offerings Lodge drum is simply "Endure!"—and without this power the dancers, by their own testimony, would never be able to finish this ordeal. The observer can gain some appreciation of this if he simply closes his eyes and stands near the entrance of the lodge during the singing. Soon the imagination sees more than the eye ever could.

INDIAN PRAYER

Nearly every Indian feast or celebration begins with a long prayer of thanks recited either in the native tongue or in English, or in a combination of the two. At times a paraphrase in English of an Indian-language prayer will be given, although many tribes are reluctant to translate their personal prayers for the white public. I will not presume here to render any such paraphrases, but in them one sees the sense of absolute dependence upon Heaven for sustenance, for family and tribal welfare, and for the well-being of those especially dear who are not present. One is reminded of Christian prayers for absent brothers and sisters.

On asking what prayer was for "the old Indians," one must generally be content simply with a description: "The old Indians had these animals and trees and rocks, and the Morning and Evening Stars, and the Sun and Moon. These things were alive, and they felt close to them and prayed to them. But white people did not understand this. They thought they were just praying to these things, but the Indians were praying to the Creator. They knew that He was there. Maybe many years ago they thought the sun and things were all there was, but the old prophets told them the truth about the Creator."

In this description, I am reminded of the strong and simply expressed feeling of prayers recorded by George Dorsey. We see here a passion for the infinite, but also an urgent plea for the things of daily life that meant so much for human well-being. And when a ritual is undertaken, we have prayers of petition such as this Rabbit Lodge prayer from 1902:

Please, Father, Man-Above, do not get impatient at our constant prayers. You caused the cedar tree to grow and from it we get leaves for our incense for this pure water.

Come and live with us, you Spirits, Supernatural-Beings, and help us in our supplications! We have boiled this water; placed the root and eating berries upon it, and it is now prepared. Poor and humble as we are in this world, surrounded by white people, please do have mercy upon us! May this cloud of smoke (incense) reach your nostrils, My Father and Grandmother! Let our circuits (the courses with the sun, during the day) be firm, and free from accidents!

My Grandfather, Big-Painted-Robe, listen to me! You are the one who directed and instructed me; and whatever I do, may it be pleasing in your sight! I have taken great pains to pursue the way which you gave me. May this woman (a wife of one participant) carry this kettle of sweet water safely to your holy place! As the geese drank that pure water without difficulty, so let it be with us! My Father, please come and be with us! [5]

[5] George A. Dorsey, *The Arapaho Sun Dance: The Ceremony of the Offerings Lodge* (Chicago: Field Columbian Museum Publication 75, Anthropological Series, Vol. IV, 1903), p. 148.

This same kind of petition, wherein the word itself is meant to share with the power of heaven, can be seen in another Sun Dance prayer, this time of the Shoshone. The translation given by Shimkin is a free approximation, and the translator believes that many Christian elements are already present, but the unique simplicity of petition is there:

> Yes, all right, My Father God, as you begin looking down toward me from above—here is now one sick. (You) having made him well, he will continue walking on this Earth. Here are we two, my dear friend and I, my future adopted relative. Now, as you keep looking toward me, (you) will bless this sick man! Now, furthermore, you will bless his children, his own woman, his own old man who are here! Also, further, that all the sick who are in this place may become well, I am praying. It is ended.[6]

Indian prayer rendered in song is verbally quite brief, and sung or chanted repeatedly, with words powerful in their simplicity. It would be impossible to detail examples here at great length. It might be informative, though, to give some instances of Indian prayer corresponding to prayers from the Christian tradition.

Praise (*Recited*):

> Grandfather Wakan-Tanka (Great Wakan)!
> You are first and always have been!
> Everything belongs to You! It is You who have created all things! You are one and alone![7]

[6] D. B. Shimkin, "The Wind River Shoshone Sun Dance," S. I., Bulletin 151 (1953), No. 41, pp. 397–484; see p. 449.

[7] Underhill, *op. cit.,* p. 202.

Praise (*Sung in major tone, solemnly*):

> I believe that in you, O heavens, dwell the ruling powers.[8]

Dream songs of ecstatic praise:

> Beloved it is good,
> He, the thunder, is saying quietly,
> it is good.   (*Pawnee*)
>
> As the wind is carrying me around the sky.
> One wind, I am master of it.   (*Chippewa*)[9]

Thanksgiving and praise (*Sung*):

> Friends, behold!
> Sacred I have been made.
> Friends, behold!
> In a sacred manner
> I have been influenced
> At the gathering of the clouds.
> Sacred I have been made,
> Friends, behold!
> Sacred I have been made.[10]

Petition (*Prayer of a Yuki shaman in a thunderstorm*):

> Please stop. My people are afraid. Why are you doing this. Father be careful. We're living here. Be easy with us. We're doing the best we can.[11]

---

[8] Densmore, *Pawnee Music*, p. 89.

[9] Densmore, "The Belief of the Indian in a Connection between Song and the Supernatural," S. I., Bulletin 151 (1953), No. 37, p. 221.

[10] Astrov, ed., *American Indian Prose and Poetry, an Anthology* (New York: John Day, 1972), p. 125.

[11] Mueller, in Krickeberg, *et al., Pre-Columbian American Religions* (New York: Holt, Rinehart and Winston, 1969), p. 226.

Petition (*For a sick boy*):

> Our Father, give this boy a good way of talking
> [talking refers to conversation with the spirits] so
> that he will be able to save our people. I want you to
> promise this to me. Please take care of this boy from
> all dangers.[12]

It is worth noting here how close to Old Testament prayer
is the familiar yet reverent way in which Indian worshipers
converse with God and His Powers. One might consider
Moses (Exodus 32) and Abraham (Genesis 18) speaking
to the Lord and cajoling, even scolding Him in their longing to receive His favor.

Propitiation or sense of need (*Sung*):

> Wa-kon-da,
> here needy he stands,
> and I am he.[13]

There do not seem to be prayers of "repentance" in traditional Indian form. The emphasis is, rather, placed on
weakness and poverty, both physical and spiritual, and not
on actual sins. But the basic sense of human need and absolute dependence is present here. As we have noted, if
there is any "sense of sin" native to Indian people, it is in
the realization that man has to break the harmony in nature by rising above and thus using his fellow animals. A
quality of human sinfulness is the failure of man to recognize how needy he is and how he must do hurt in order

[12] *Ibid.*, p. 227.
[13] Astrov, *op. cit.*, p. 135.

to fill his own needs. Indian songs of propitiation make one aware of this condition. The songs of various peyote people, mingled with Native and Christian elements, do show us the repentance-nature of that rite, and again, the spiritual poverty that leads them to pray in such a manner as recorded by Ruth Underhill:

> Now we begin
> I look to you.
> Look on me and on these people.
> Help us as we meet here.
> *Song of the Road Man*[14]

SUFFERING AND RELIGIOUS EXPERIENCE

Among the plains tribes, one is made conscious of the constant Indian awareness of suffering by the conversation of the Indian women, who generally do all the hard labor connected with providing food and other necessities for the Sun Dance and various ceremonies. It is mother, grandmother, sister, and wife who must work to prepare their men for the ceremony and sustain them in it. Here, for a brief time, the old tribal division of labor returns. As in the days of war and hunt, the men must endure intense physical suffering—for the people. The women must work long and tirelessly—for the people. A middle-aged Christian woman was commenting on her role here—caring for several grandchildren, a sick mother, and an aged grandmother, while laboring at the task of cooking (a function

---

[14] Underhill, *op. cit.,* p. 267.

with ritual significance)—to supply the sponsors and the dancers in their concluding feast. At the question, "Do you think it's all worth it?" the weary reply was, "Yes, I think so." And this belief was illuminated as she went on to describe the experience of suffering which her sons and the other participants underwent. She thought their faces, covered by crowns of sage and painted in such a way as to heighten their drawn appearance, looked like the face of Christ in His passion.

A careless interpretation here can convey an impression of masochism. Perhaps sometimes there was an element of this; but again, one notes how "functional" such asceticism was. To do without food and water was the usual lot of the Indians, especially on the plains. To endure the sun and other elements had to become second nature. The threat of possible ritual torture, if they were captured by enemies, was often present to these men. Actually, the disappearance of warfare as a way of life *has* altered the element of ascetic suffering in many Indian rites, and has even eliminated for many tribes the sham battle formerly connected with cutting down the tree for the lodge pole.

If the suffering of ascetic self-denial is a religious experience, one can perhaps better understand the incredible capacity of the historical Indian tribes to endure the near genocide undergone for some three hundred years. As observed earlier, the Indian's religion alone (including its very humorous sides) has helped him so far to survive the rude culture shock that has not yet come to an end—in many ways parallel to the suffering which has been religiously interpreted among the Jewish people. Similarly St. Paul made *thlipsis,* or "tribulation," almost a mark by which the genuine Christian community could be identified.

Much ink, and perhaps a bit of artistic embellishment, has been spent trying to perpetuate the classic patience of the faces of old Indians. And yet, the picture remains by and large true, and suggests again how suffering has tempered the Indian spirit. Certainly Indians have not been passive before their conquerors, nor are they today. In the nineteenth century many tribes waged some of the fiercest opposition ever known to military history, and in our own time many Indians have become formidable political fighters as well. But through it all has been displayed an ability to endure and to relate this endurance to the land, to the Powers, and to the Great Spirit. Some small movements, like the Warriors of the Rainbow, have preached that Indian suffering has been a purifying force in Indian history, thus strengthening them to be the forgers of a world brotherhood. With such examples in mind, this chapter concludes with some prayers and other signs of the spiritual strength that suffering has produced in the Indian character over the ages. I do not include examples from Black Elk, whose personal legacy is already widely known.

Let us begin with the song of a warrior:

I shall vanish and be no more,
But the land over which I now roam
Shall remain.
And change not.[15]

The confrontation with destiny and death, and the resigned spirit of acceptance became part of the cry of Chief White Antelope, as he and the other ancestors of our Chey-

[15] Astrov, *op. cit.*, p. 133.

enne and Arapaho people fell helpless beneath the cavalry
hooves in the betrayal at Sand Creek:

> Nothing lives long
> Only the earth and the mountains.[16]

A Dakota Sioux version of the same type of resignation
goes:

> The old men say
> the earth only endures
> you spoke truly
> you are right.[17]

The spirit of the plains is expressed in another song:

> In all lands
> adventures I seek
> hence amid hardships I have walked.[18]

And tribulation, as St. Paul wrote, produces hope. Out of
the trials of the nineteenth-century nightmare came these
brief songs of hope which, though temporarily and bitterly
frustrated, continue now as aspirations for a better world
order:

> The Father will descend,
> The earth will tremble,
> Everybody will arise,
> Stretch out your hands.

[16] This version is quoted in Dee Brown, *Bury My Heart at Wounded
Knee,* p. 89.
[17] Densmore, *Teton Sioux Music,* S. I., Bulletin 61, p. 340.
[18] *Ibid.,* p. 340.

The Crow—Ehe'eye!
I saw him when he flew down,
To the earth, to the earth.
He has renewed our life.
He has taken pity on us.

We shall live again,
We shall live again.[19]

The religious experience of aspiration to a new order grows amid the trials and sufferings of those who endure it. Harry Paige, in his *Songs of the Teton Sioux,* describes how the old people still see hope, even after the first battle of Wounded Knee, in the wind that blows over the grass every spring. The very landscape, too, has become a part of the impatience for divine help that pervades the temperament of the plains Indians. As one studies a section of the Wind River Mountains, he will observe the outline of a profile which, say the Indian people, represents a sleeping Indian. He has slept for a long time now, they say, but someday he will rise again.

[19] Astrov, *op. cit.,* p. 144.

Chapter Five

An Indian Christianity?

Brother, we do not wish to destroy your religion, or take it from you; we only want to enjoy our own.

Brother, we are told that you have been preaching to white people in this place; these people are our neighbors, we are acquainted with them; we will wait a little while and see what effect your preaching has upon them. If we find it does them good, makes them honest, and less disposed to cheat Indians, we will then consider again what you have said.[1]

Seneca Chief Red Jacket to a missionary, 1805

For it has seemed good to the Holy Spirit and to us to lay upon you no greater burden than these necessary things: that you abstain from what has been sacrificed to idols and from blood and from what is strangled and from unchastity. If you keep yourselves from these, you will do well. . . .

Letter from the Apostles to Gentile Converts,
Acts 15:28–29

Granting good will on the part of all parties concerned where Indian tribal religion meets the Christian preaching of missionaries, at what point is it apparent that an insolu-

---

[1] Astrov, ed., *American Indian Prose and Poetry, an Anthology* (New York: John Day, 1972), p. 164.

ble conflict has been reached? As the epigraph for this
chapter I have quoted part of an address by an Indian chief
to a Christian missionary. The remainder of the speech is
a gentle and perplexed question as to why the missionary,
a member of a race already guilty of injustice and a Church
already bitterly divided, should want to convert Indians
from a religion that was given them by their forefathers
as a way to worship, love one another, and be united. It is
recorded that the preacher refused the hand of friendship
because there was no fellowship between his "religion of
God" and the Indians' "works of the devil." In turn, I have
cited a letter resulting from a controversy among the early
Christians about Gentile converts to a Church as yet made
up mostly of Jews. The decision, as the letter points out,
was that the Church should not lay on the shoulders of new
converts more than the most necessary cultural and moral
burdens—in this case to avoid food sacrificed to idols and
blood, as well as forms of impurity probably common
among Gentiles of the time.

Every tradition has its ethical norms and cultural teachings, the most basic of which one assumes appeal to a common human notion of right and wrong. Each tradition
tries to adjust to contemporary needs while retaining the
core that is essential to its self-identity. What was a mystery
to the Indians was, of course, that the Christian religion
contained missionary teaching as part of its mandate, and
that this religion seemed to serve, in spite of the enthusiastic proselytizing, as such poor "medicine" for so many of
its adherents. There is little point to going into the matter
of the perennial discrepancy between saying and doing.
The real problem is: What does Christianity offer that
makes it unique, and what essentials, if any, must one sacrifice of his own culture in order to embrace it? Many In-

dians, especially among the youth and young middle-aged, have already rejected Christianity as being a white man's religion, and have either ceased all religious practices or have returned to the tribal religion in its contemporary form.

Even Vine Deloria, Jr., as this book is being written, has announced his own categorical renunciation of Christianity, not for any of the accidentals, but simply because of its very basic concept of linear time, which he holds to be foreign and destructive to the Native American worldview. And yet, many Indians do not share this radical viewpoint. In this chapter we shall investigate whether there must be any conflict in basic beliefs and practice between those various traditions and essential Christianity.

We have seen how the basics of religion are present in most ancient North American traditions: at least a primitive but highly refined notion of God (developed over centuries of meditation and outside contact), belief in man's creaturehood, the practice of prayer and sacrifice, ethical consciousness, a belief in life after death, and elaborate sacred ritual. In some cases there may be irreconcilable differences between tribal practices and one or another alleged teaching of Christianity. One may leave it to those in various locales, who have closer knowledge of the situation, to specify the differences: whether, for example, the various Indian arts of "doctoring" are compatible with Christianity is an open question, though from personal accounts it would seem that these arts, while not accepted by medical practitioners, are not for that reason anti-Christian. Certainly, where unquestioned sorcery and malevolent black magic might be practiced, the Christian must separate himself from them.

In recent years some efforts have been made to situate worship of Christ within Indian culture. Peripheral examples of this would be the wearing of Indian-style vestments and ceremonial bonnets at religious services, as well as participation by clergy in prayers of the Sun Dance and other ceremonies. More centrally, the New Testament has been translated into Indian symbols or even the native tongue. Missionaries often pray with replicas of the Sacred Pipe and the symbolism connected with it. Some work is being done to render the Lord's Prayer and eucharistic prayers in terms of Indian symbolism. I recently took part in a Catholic service for the national Day of Indian Prayer, and found it promising, as did many of the Indians who attended. The thirty-five-minute service (quite brief for an Indian ceremony) began with a recording in the native language: "Fear not: you do not have to be afraid, or fear the dark. God gave His Son to give us life so we can live. All will be good again. God loves you, will take care of you, make you strong, hold you, make you well again."

There followed an incensation of the people with the traditional cedar incense, and then a recitation of the Lord's Prayer by the priest-celebrant in English, using Indian symbolism, while an elderly Indian recited it in the tribal language. Next, a practice common to both traditions: the recitation of a litany of prayers for the dead, the sick, and the suffering. A traditional Christian hymn was then sung, followed by readings from Galatians and John's Gospel on unity in the Spirit. Next was a prayer of praise of God, using a combination of Old Testament psalmody and Indian panegyric of creation. Impromptu prayers were next said by the celebrant and then by members of the congregation, followed by the traditional Benediction of the

Blessed Sacrament, which is still well received in many Indian churches.

Whether such efforts as these—which must go deeper still—will maintain or build a living Indian Christianity is not presently clear. It is a fact that for many years a great number of Indians saw the dedicated people on Christian missions as islands of light amid great desolation. So it was with the Flathead delegation that came from Montana to St. Louis seeking out the great missionary DeSmet a century and a half ago. In many cases, Indians did not really identify missionaries with other "Whites" at all. Such acceptance and trust is not so common any longer, for reasons evident to those who witness current events. Members of the American Indian Movement on some reservations have explicitly told the missionaries to leave. Other groups have simply taken an attitude of nonviolent rejection. But one might presume that it is simply the *whiteness* of Christian missions that these groups want to see disappear, at least in the case of more moderate Indians. If this is the case, supposing there can be a tradition that is truly Indian and truly Christian, what needs to be done? First, we should understand the present situation.

ALIENATION

The word "alienation" is used here very deliberately, not just to describe a vague feeling of separation but in the Marxist sense: the Indian has been expropriated of what is a very part of him by his birthright, and so lives virtually in a foreign country—symbolized by the reservation agency or the urban relocation situation. Hence the reaction either of passive hostility or of open revolutionary activity. There is no need to detail the matter of American government bungling of Indian affairs, both past and present. Dee Brown's *Bury My Heart at Wounded Knee* does this with excellent documentation. John Collier's book, *Indians of the Americas,* is written largely from personal experience with the Bureau of Indian Affairs. Vine Deloria, Jr., has already pointed out some of the mistakes church people have made that contributed to what he calls the "cultural vacuum."

In order to realize how deeply culture determines the quality of worship, I again ask the Christian reader to consider his own environment of worship; what he has come to expect in language, music, art, architecture, external signs. When any of these are changed too suddenly or radically, his security is jolted. This intrusion of alien elements into one's at-homeness is a small sample of the great Indian cultural trauma. The most violent upheaval in culture actually took place for most tribes within the space of one or two generations, as conquerors of British, French, and Spanish origin swept over their domains and made them foreigners in their own territories.

One often hears laments today about the moral fiber of Indian society and how weak it has become—though one might seriously question whether it has decayed as badly as that of white America. But granting the premise, what might be the reasons for it? To begin with, all the formal education Indian children received was through fireside instruction by their elders, given in the native tongue by means of stories. If such a child is taken at the age of five or six and placed in a government or church boarding school where the Indian language is forbidden and all cultural practices interdicted, and then sent home for summers, and, finally, relocated in the heart of a large city, it is not difficult to imagine the resultant confusion of value training.

It has been easy for middle-class white people to comment on the poor condition of Indian homes on a reservation, and to be upset at the presence of abandoned cars, beer cans, and the like; but if one considers how the Indian's highly natural sense of living off the land was suddenly replaced by a technocratic revolution from which he was excluded, the picture clears up somewhat. People must use the implements of technology to survive, but alienation still makes itself felt in that the training for use of these things to improve the *quality* of life has not made proportionate progress.

I have often heard it seriously asked—at the time of this writing just recently by the master of ceremonies of a popular night talk-show—whether there is something in the Indian's makeup, physiological or psychological, that "can't handle alcohol." To give a serious response to such a question, one can again begin with the religious aspect —the sudden bestowal of an amazing liquid that sent the consciousness soaring. The Sioux called the white man's whiskey *minne wakan*—"holy water" or "mysterious water" permeated with strange power to affect the human mind. Among a people so instinctively religious and "power oriented," the effects of such an innovation could be, and were, disastrous. More than one psychologist, including William James, has suggested that the drunken consciousness is but an aspect of the religious consciousness —as the strongly religious orientation of Alcoholics Anonymous might confirm. But from the beginning there has been a strong element of social psychology or learning involved too. Liquor came to the Indian people in North America thrown to them by troopers from the palisades of a fort or handed over in crocks as exchange for valuable pelts, or even given with the express purpose of rendering them incapable of resistance. Combine this history of the past with the present atmosphere on reservations of idleness and boredom, along with enforced social inferiority, and the drinking problem too takes on new dimensions.

From all that has been said of family customs and child-rearing, especially in its ritual context, it is not hard to understand why Indian family life has so often suffered fragmentation. One cannot let a father's identity as protector, huntsman (this is less true of the agricultural tribes, and their easier assimilation illustrates it in some cases), and religious leader be snatched from him and still expect to see a strong, confident family head. When the Indian woman, "liberated" far more by this upheaval than she generally desires, is forced to do the bread-winning by hard labor, the resultant effects in a young boy's life and self-image are predictable. A girl will not be so anxious to follow her mother in marriage, and may, rather, simply have a child out of wedlock—a rare occurrence in ancient tribal life, apparently—often leaving the mother, now grandmother, to care for the child.

Finally, returning to the specifically religious issue, there is an extensive history of ridicule and condescension toward Indian rites and customs by white missionaries. This was not invariably the case, as many sensitive and intelligent clergy and mission workers strove to learn the Indian language and to incorporate Indian customs into worship; but there was more than enough misinterpretation and denunciation to drive the customs into the hills with the old holy men, where they generally remain today, emerging at times for special feasts, but practiced away from white observation. This leaves the Indian "layman" to attend a kind of worship that is not really his "parish" structure, and to respond in song and prayer forms that are not his own.

WHY CHRISTIANITY?

I write this section clearly ignorant about what will happen to organized Christianity among Indian peoples. At present it is certainly a sign of contradiction, though, I would judge, not quite yet the kind of contradiction intended by the Gospel writers. As consciousness-raising increases among Indian people—and it is doing so rapidly, especially among the young—anything that has come from the white conqueror is met with suspicion and even hatred. And yet, hatred is rarely an ingredient in Indian traditions; a warring and vengeful tradition perhaps, but not one of enduring hatred. Among those Indians who are rediscovering their cultural identity by returning to the old religious practices are also many who have been touched by Christian sources as well. How this may resolve itself was brought home to me during a conversation with a young Indian woman, a former student who is now a highly effective social worker and educator. We had talked about how previously many Catholic Indians had stayed away from Indian practices because the missionaries forbade them to attend. I remarked that now the Church is not likely to try to lay down such prohibitions. The quite matter-of-fact response, given without rancor, was "The Church can't get away with orders like that anymore, Father." A far cry this, from the plaint I had heard once in the past, in another time and place, "Oh, I wish I wasn't an Indian!"

Ruth Underhill divides modern Indian prophets into "hostile prophets" and "prophets of co-existence." Among the "hostiles" she includes Smohalla, Wodzuwob, and Wovoka, while among the "co-existents" are Handsome Lake (Ganioda'yo) of the Iroquois, the Indian Shakers, and the peyote followers.[2] Generally the lines seem to have been drawn inasmuch as the Indian people experienced either hypocrisy or genuine love and valiant effort and personal witness at the hands of white missionaries. However, it is important to note that many of the hostile prophets were more Christian in their basic inspiration and teachings than some of the prophets of coexistence. Thus, Wovoka employed far more Christian beliefs in his apocalyptic than did Handsome Lake in his reform, a fact which confirms the view that often the common denominator of these prophets was not the faith but the foreign culture involved in its transmission.

There are Wovokas and Handsome Lakes today on nearly every reservation and in many urban groups. The Wovokas are, of course, represented by some of the more militant members of the American Indian Movement, though obviously they are not likely to try to precipitate a universal cataclysm based on divine revelation. More common to antichurch Indians is the conciliatory attitude of Handsome Lake, "the Iroquois St. Paul" as Werner Mueller called him. This early-nineteenth-century Seneca religious leader experienced a vision in 1799 at the age of fifty-five, and was converted from a life of drunkenness and apathy to one of Indian apostleship. For fifteen years he traveled about preaching a return to the Indian traditions, but at the same time discouraging obsolete practices. He

[2] Underhill, *Red Man's Religion* (Chicago: University of Chicago Press, 1965), pp. 254-269.

stressed the sovereignty of the One God, Hawenijo, over all subordinate divinities, and especially over Haninseano, the evil spirit. Many of the old dances that involved flirting with evil spirits were converted into mere social entertainments, and worship became directed toward the Creator. Many ethnological accounts emphasize how powerful was the influence of Ganioda'yo on his and neighboring peoples.[3]

Such history as this brings up the question, "Who is dialoguing with whom, and what doctrine is challenging what doctrine?" The Judeo-Christian tradition *has* made its mark on Indian religion, whichever direction Native Americans decide to go in the future; perhaps we see here the promise that the Word of God is always going to be heard, through and maybe in spite of human preachers; Jesus too preached the Word in proportion as people were able to receive it (cf. Mark 4:33). Handsome Lake is generally considered to have been influenced by the powerful biblical notion of the Father-God and by much of the Old Testament teaching against idolatry.

Among the Pueblo there exist, side by side, the various nature cults and a fully traditional Catholicism, with certain syncretic practices tolerated or even encouraged by the church authorities. What subtle influences one tradition may have had on another can be judged only by those with firsthand acquaintance. The peyote religion, as is well known, is one of the most enthusiastic of Jesus cults. His name figures in their prayers and He is symbolized by the plant itself, being made present by its "power."

The Sun Dances of the Arapaho and the Shoshone are now filled with Christian traits. It is believed by some eth-

[3] For details, see Krickeberg, *et al.*, *Pre-Columbian American Religions* (New York: Holt, Rinehart and Winston, 1969), pp. 186ff.

nologists that the influence of the Episcopal bishop John Roberts can be seen in the works of charity and gifting that occur in the Shoshone celebration (although this could also be related to Arapaho custom), as well as the great attention paid to God as personal Creator and Father. Arapaho Offerings Lodge worshipers can be seen to wear scapulars, rosaries, and medals about their necks, and Christian symbols on their beaded aprons. Recent tradition says that each participant over the three-day period should dance to each one of the twelve side poles, which now represent the apostles in their positions around the Center, Christ. The belief of some tribes, like the Shoshone, that the pole also bears the ailments of the tribe supports the ease with which it might be identified with the Servant of God who bears our iniquities.

Some purists may pejoratively call all of this syncretism, but to do so would be to deride the testimony of the centuries and the cultures from Syria to Gaul to the New World which have influenced Christian teaching and ritual and intertwined with it to create new indigenous forms of church worship. Rather than mock such "syncretism," one might encourage these native additions as genuine worship, while advocating (as do many peyote leaders today) participation in the usual forms of Christian devotion and education.

Perhaps one should have more trust that the Powers for good will draw fruit from these cultural interminglings. There is a legend about some tribal creation myths that when man, or the first man and woman, were on their raft amid the waters of the flood, there was a cross present with them. We know that the cross is a prominent Indian symbol, from the plains to the east coast, and no doubt in the past depicted the sacred Four Corners, which in turn stand for divine providence and care for the earth and for mankind. Yet here we have the belief of Christian Indians who know both their own myths and Christian doctrine. What the Creator and Father might intend through a long-range use of symbolism is a mystery to all of us, but we must handle it with care.

What further value might Christian proclamation have for Indians today? We might suggest that at present the provisional role of political liberation be considered. By liberation I mean the work of freeing people from social bondage to live the good life, so that they might then seek to reconcile their deeper spiritual alienation. Paulo Freire has emphasized the need for theology to take anthropology as its starting point. Theology, wroter Freire, exercises its task as servant of the gospel only when it assists liberation, or when it aids the realization that man *is* being freed by God's intervention. In this, the gospel is carrying out its work of "conscientization."

When it is faithful to its commission, theology counter-balances the naïveté that so often accompanies religious experience, and opens one to a vision of faith that has no fear of cultural differences. One way in which Christian theology can aid the liberation of the oppressed is by finally confessing to the dignity of those traditions from which the oppressed have often been snatched by main force. For a sense of one's own history is part of the sense of personal and communal dignity, which liberates through equalization.

Equally important is Christianity's fundamental duty to preach the necessary conditions for liberation: repentance and atonement. Man is called to be at one with his Creator through being at one with his fellow human beings and with nature. If he is going to the altar to offer his gift and there he remembers that his brother had something against him, he must first return and be reconciled to his brother before returning to offer his gift. It helps to recall that the Greek word for "reconcile" here includes the notion of "becoming something other" than what one was. The call to reconciliation and atonement lies first on the shoulders of Whites in our society, but it resonates remarkably with the traditional Indian sense of universal integrity.

On the level of fundamental theological teachings, Christianity might continue to be of help to Indian tradition as well as to Christian Indians themselves, not by destroying but by fulfilling—as theological reflection on the gospel develops. I would stress here, first, the place of Jesus as a person in the human psychological and historical sense, and as God incarnate; second, a developed doctrine of sin and redemption; and third, Christian love, or agapē.

The Person of Jesus

I have remarked above how often the name of Jesus comes up in Indian prayers, even outside the conventional liturgical scene. Indians have so deep a reverence for a sacred and heroic figure, for a prophet, that scholars such as Joachim Wach have regarded Indians as having the loftiest of religious traditions among all primitive societies. Again, Ignatius Loyola, who in his *Spiritual Exercises* devotes three weeks to contemplating the entire public life of Jesus of Nazareth, would find the Indian contemplative spirit fertile ground for the Word—as in fact the *Jesuit Relations* so often testify. Always strongly motivated to endure pain and hardship, Indians today find in Jesus a preeminent model for imitation. His desert fast is now an encouragement for the Sun Dance and other vigils; His labors for those who must bear the burdens of providing for the festival; His face on the cross for those who pray during their third day of hunger and thirst, dancing to the Center Pole. And much to the point for our times, lest one see here only a passive asceticism, Jesus' Sermon on the Mount and other moral teachings have become an integral part of the message of liberation.

Jesus as God Incarnate

Beyond question, the whole doctrine of God becoming man is a paradox to the rational mind. Traditional Indian teaching, however, thrives on paradox, as witness the mysterious interchange of animal and human and divine identities. For modern Indians, no doubt, the paradox may become more jarring, at least as many younger Indians now find it. And this is fitting enough, since there is nothing gained by artificially paralleling the ancient myths of heroes and demigods with the Incarnation. This had already been attempted by primitive Gnosticism. The fact is, *no* human culture can receive the Incarnation without being shocked and stunned by its reality. But what is valuable in Indian tradition is the readiness to live with contradictions, to accept the mental anguish they often entail, without trying to solve them by intellectual apologetics. If the paradox of the Incarnation is shown to be redemptive and salvific "medicine" (*not* just for Indians) which makes for a better life and better witness, it will be embraced by religious Indians with great devotion.

Sin and Redemption

I have already discussed sin and redemption in some detail earlier. Let me simply add here that no word has ever caused as much turmoil, in both the provocation and the reaction, as the word "sin." Christians envision, in many instances, the teaching on sin as a heavy-hanging cudgel of moral persuasion over the head of humanity, or as a source of nagging guilt and crippling scrupulosity. If this is the correct doctrine, there is no place for it in the Indian tradition. But such a notion is a distortion. Even if one holds to the notion of "hereditary" guilt, this should not entail traditional imagery such as hellfire. In fact, Indian mythology does understand an idea of the effects that one ancestor can have on his descendants, as witness the assertion of the legend that one person may decree that other men should, in future generations, have to die: human solidarity is bound up with the notion of a common origin. If one takes the first eleven chapters of Genesis as simply an account of how mankind rebels against God, Indian teaching in general finds nothing uncongenial here. Indians have always been ready to recognize the evil in themselves and in others, and this not merely in the innocuous form of a "human-condition" theory, but as the presence of a readiness to do evil things.

Correlative to the teaching on sin, a teaching on redemption, whether it be by vicarious suffering taken on by God himself out of love, or by the transforming life of Christ, or even by the simile of liberation of a slave, would seem to speak directly to the Indian mentality. That man is saved by grace and faith would be of value and a help to religious Indians where overemphasis may be placed on human means to attain favors or visions from God. This should, of course, not exclude the kind of mind-opening asceticism discussed earlier, but it can be a comforting and freeing doctrine that could contribute to a more perservering day-to-day asceticism in which the trials of life become occasions of being closer to God.

Agapē

The meaning of *agapē* in the New Testament is unique. To speak of an utterly selfless love as Jesus and Paul do is finally a stumbling-block to the understanding of all cultures and all persons. While Indian religion certainly calls for generosity and self-sacrifice—a touching example of this can be seen in Black Elk's description of the great Chief Crazy Horse in *Black Elk Speaks*—it is finally no more secure in the face of the summons to love as God has loved us than is any other human tradition. Like other cultures which profess belief in the High God, Indian culture did not appreciate the nature of a personal, here-and-now supreme God whose very existence is personal love. But this is not surprising, for self-analysis shows that there has to be an element of self in even the most generous actions, and absolutely selfless loving is beyond human comprehension.

Agapē has its cosmic implications as well. If a person or group can reach out for this universal and non-self-serving charity, what St. Paul says of Christ begins to happen: in Christ there is neither Jew nor Greek, slave nor free, Barbarian nor Scythian, male nor female. Differences remain, but unjust discrimination disappears. Faith is thus not identified with the aspirations of one culture for power and prestige—as Kierkegaard preached to his countrymen, who seemed to believe that to be a good Dane was to be a good Christian. The implications of loving faith apply to tribal cultures as well (although their aspirations have seldom been as arrogant as the claims of Western mega-nations). Thus the African historian John Mbiti writes of his fear of a new assertion of tribalism and African nationalism in emerging African nations, and he urges Christianity as the antidote to the hatred that might arise from an otherwise justified racial pride and identity.[4] This same message could apply to American Indians, as the new raising of consciousness restores to them legitimate pride in their traditions. Blending together a sense of self-worth and charity is what the gospel witness is all about.

FOR A LIVING INDIAN CHRISTIANITY

If Indian religious tradition is to become one of the great cultural manifestations of the Christian life, rather than simply a pastiche of certain attractive practices and teachings, many areas of growth are indicated. Before everything else, as we have seen, there must be less discrepancy between preaching and practice. Indians are far readier, I believe, to accept the human failings of others than are most people, but if the proclamation of the gospel is not attended by empathetic understanding and charity, it will preach only to a stanch few. Second, as Chief Joseph of the Nez Percé and many other Indians have asked, if Chris-

[4] John S. Mbiti, *African Religions and Philosophy* (Garden City, N.Y.: Doubleday and Co., 1969), pp. 350 ff.

tians cannot get together among themselves over the meaning of the gospel message, why should others care to join
their divided sects? The practice of parceling out reservation areas to different religious groups according to someone's arbitrary choice could never strike the proposed converts as anything but cynical. Indian tribes and intertribal
groups now seek fellowship with the churches for one purpose: their own place in society, the Church, and the brotherhood of man. Dialogue with "third partners" such as this
should help the Christian churches in the movement toward Christian unity.

A more difficult problem for an Indian Christianity
would be the question of the real Indian involvement once
proposed by Deloria. First of all, cultural adaptation of
mission churches will have to go much deeper than it has.
The catechesis of the young, for example, might take the
form of story-telling as of old, in evenings at home, including tribal leaders as well as catechists, unless tribal leaders
can fill both roles. Indian worship in the form of Sun
Dance, Sweat Lodge, and even the peyote cult might be
given positive recognition. Eucharistic liturgies might become more real centers of tribal gathering, with feasting
and socializing as a supplement. The management of
church funds and charitable works should ideally be carried on through Native tribal agencies rather than by the
church collections, or else integrated with tribal social action.

These proposals are ideals, and we cannot be deceived
about their difficulty of attainment. First, there is often a
tribal tradition that only a very few select holy men and
their assistants should be "professional" religionists, while
others simply follow. Thus, any broad extension of the
Christian ministry to include permanent deacons such as

exist in the Episcopal and Roman Catholic churches, or Indian ministers of other denominations, faces serious obstacles. Persons trained for and given such a privileged position face severe pressure and possibly widespread apathy or rejection. Also, Indian tribes, being clannish by nature, are not free of that natural jealousy attendant upon such an environment. In this, it is the demanding task of those who are already Christians to encourage the same spirit in *all* church matters—that of solidarity and cooperation—that one sees in the periodic functions of Indian tribal worship.

Whatever solutions may be arrived at, if Christianity is to remain a vital force among Indians, the Church of Vatican II and the World Council will have to continue to distance itself from all remnants of the condescension of early white arrivals in America, from the hate-filled spite of a Cotton Mather, and from the unexamined rigidity of seventeenth-century Rome, when the cultural adaptations of missionaries to China were terminated. Arnold Toynbee once said of the tragic conclusion to the Ricci experiment in China that this was where the Church lost once and for all the opportunity to become truly catholic. The present issue is whether Toynbee's words symbolize a declaration of fact or a challenge.

Bibliography

Among the extensive number of works on Indian culture, I have tried here to stress those which discuss religion more specifically. For those who may wish to do reading in the more technical anthropological works, I recommend, first, the entire series of Smithsonian Institution, Bureau of American Ethnology Bulletins, which begin in 1889, and can be ordered, if available, from the United States Government Printing Office, Washington, D.C. Second, many old works may still be obtainable from the Field Columbian Museum, Chicago, or through the Kraus Reprint Corporation. Finally, publications in the American Museum of Natural History Anthropological Papers, New York, may still be available in many cases.

Alexander, Hartley Burr. *North American Mythology*. Cambridge, Mass.: University Press, 1916.

———. *The World's Rim: Great Mysteries of the North American Indians*. Lincoln: University of Nebraska Press, 1969.

Astrov, Margot, ed. *American Indian Prose and Poetry, an Anthology*. New York: John Day, 1946, 1972.

Black Elk (with John G. Neihardt). *Black Elk Speaks*. Lincoln: University of Nebraska Press, 1961 (from 1932).

—— (with Joseph Epes Brown). *The Sacred Pipe: Black Elk's Account of the Seven Rites of the Oglala Sioux.* Norman: University of Oklahoma, 1970.

Brown, Dee. *Bury My Heart at Wounded Knee.* New York: Holt, Rinehart and Winston, 1971.

Cash, Joseph H., and Hoover, Herbert T. *To Be an Indian: An Oral History.* New York: Holt, Rinehart and Winston, 1971. Interviews with Indian people.

Collier, John. *Indians of the Americas.* New York: Mentor Books, 1947.

Deloria, Vine, Jr. *Custer Died for Your Sins, an Indian Manifesto.* New York: Macmillan, 1969.

——. *God Is Red.* New York: Grosset and Dunlap, 1973. A summons to Indians to return to the old religions and to reject Christianity as a foreign intruder, with a suggestion to Whites to learn from Indian tradition. This book, appearing during the writing of the present work, shows a more and more radicalized Deloria.

——. *We Talk, You Listen.* New York: Macmillan, 1970.

Krickeberg, Walter, *et al. Pre-Columbian American Religions,* trans. Stanley Davis. New York: Holt, Rinehart and Winston, 1969.

LaBarre, Weston. *The Peyote Cult.* Hamden, Conn.: The Shoestring Press, enlarged edition, 1964.

Mails, Thomas E. *The Mystic Warriors of the Plains.* Garden City, N.Y.: Doubleday and Co., 1972. A large, attractive edition profusely illustrated with paintings by the author.

Marriot, Alice, and Rachlin, Carol K. *American Indian Mythology.* New York: Thomas Y. Crowell, 1968. These are accounts taken from interviews with Indian people.

Paige, Harry W. *Songs of the Teton Sioux.* Los Angeles: Westernlore Press, 1970. Contains an account of the Ghost Dance movement and translations of Sioux religious and entertainment music.

Prucha, Francis Paul, ed. *The Indian in American History.* New York: Holt, Rinehart and Winston, 1971.

Radin, Paul. *The Story of the American Indian.* New York: Liveright Publishing Co., 1944. A popular work by one of the great American ethnologists.

Shakespeare, Tom. *The Sky People.* New York: The Vantage Press, 1971. This book is written by an Arapaho Indian with a family tradition of Indian knowledge and lore, and a good knowledge of anthropology.

Starkloff, Carl. "American Indian Religion and Christianity: Confrontation and Dialogue." In Marty, Martin E., and Peerman, Dean, *New Theology No. 9,* New York: Macmillan, 1972, pp. 121–150. A shorter study, preliminary to the present effort to discuss the subject theologically.

Trenholm, Virginia Cole. *The Arapahoes, Our People.* Norman: University of Oklahoma Press, 1970.

Trenholm, Virginia Cole, and Maurine Carley. *The Shoshones. Sentinals of the Rockies.* Norman: University of Oklahoma Press, 1969.

Underhill, Ruth M. *Red Man's America.* Chicago: University of *Chicago Press,* 1971.

———. *Red Man's Religion.* Chicago: University of Chicago Press, 1972. An excellent and sensitive account of basic concepts and traditions, with contemporary comments.